Crw.

Talbot Prize

1937

THE MOUNTAIN SCENE

I

THE MOUNTAIN SCENE

BY

F. S. SMYTHE

WITH SEVENTY-EIGHT REPRODUCTIONS OF
PHOTOGRAPHS BY THE AUTHOR

ADAM AND CHARLES BLACK
4, 5 AND 6 SOHO SQUARE LONDON W1
1937

A crevasse near the Bergli]

Australia and New Zealand
THE OXFORD UNIVERSITY PRESS, MELBOURNE
Canada
THE MACMILLAN COMPANY OF CANADA, TORONTO
South Africa
THE OXFORD UNIVERSITY PRESS, CAPE TOWN
India, Burma, China and F.M.S.
MACMILLAN AND COMPANY LIMITED
BOMBAY   CALCUTTA   MADRAS

MADE AND PRINTED IN GREAT BRITAIN
LETTERPRESS BY THE WHITEFRIARS PRESS LTD. LONDON AND TONBRIDGE
PHOTOGRAVURE PLATES BY HARRISON AND SONS LTD. LONDON AND HIGH WYCOMBE

PREFACE

THE photographs in this book are intended to serve a dual purpose : to interest those who enjoy the hills, and to illustrate points in the art and technique of mountain photography which it is hoped may be of service to all those who like to bring back some pictorial record of their wanderings on the hills. In some cases, however, photographs have been included merely to forge a link in the story of an expedition. There is, for instance, nothing of pictorial appeal in the ice wall of Kangchenjunga, yet the story of the Kangchenjunga Expedition would be incomplete without a photograph of it.

Having read nothing myself about the finer points of photography, and making no claim to be anything but an amateur of the art, I suspect that my more expert friends will disagree violently with the opinions set forth in the preliminary chapter. Perhaps in defence I can say that the errors so sadly obvious in many of these photographs will stimulate many with the desire to improve upon them and their own work.

I have chosen photographs of pictorial, i.e. static, rather than human interest, though the mountaineer himself finds a place in many. Climbing photographs are legion and the study of the human form in all its manifold positions on a mountainside deserves a volume to itself.

When apparatus or photographic materials have proved their excellence I have not hesitated to mention them by name, though I have no financial interest in the firms concerned.

The four photographs taken on Mount Everest have been included by courtesy of the Mount Everest Committee.

CONTENTS

vii

THE MOUNTAIN SCENE

PHOTOGRAPHING THE HILLS

Most who visit the hills and rejoice in natural scenery, whether they be walkers or mountaineers, like to take home with them some record of their wanderings. Years afterwards, when memories are failing, a photograph will recapture much that has long been forgotten. And it will do more than this; it will extend the scope of memory far beyond one particular scene and set in motion a whole train of thoughts, just as a smell may resurrect some childhood scene. Even an old print faded and underexposed can do this, but it goes almost without saying that the better the photograph the more vivid the memory, for a well-taken picture has the power of recalling not only form and detail but many other qualities, such as colour, sound and smell; it may even be interesting to someone else, though he is a bold or tactless fellow (like myself) who parades his album for his friends' inspection.

Fine scenery deserves fine photography, yet how many make the least attempt to master even the underlying principles of photography? They are content to point their camera indiscriminately and hope for the best, and the result is often the worst. They believe, and the old traditions die hard, that elaborate equipment and a long apprenticeship to the craft are necessary to produce a really fine photograph, and that pictures, such as adorn the walls of photographic exhibitions, can only be taken by professionals with life-long experience. Those who take successful photographs are often asked how they do it, and if they reply that the simplest apparatus was used and that even that complicated and terrifying manœuvre known as a time-exposure was avoided they are greeted with frank incredulity. Of the 78 photographs in this book only two or three were not instantaneous exposures, and the great majority were nothing but ordinary snapshots taken with simple and cheap pocket cameras. Doubtless my more expert friends will reply that the pictures look like it, and I shall be reminded of an amusing experience near Zermatt. I was walking up a path to a hut when I came across an old gentleman half buried in an enormous dark cloth, crouching like a beast of prey behind a monstrous full-plate camera weighing I should think at least thirty pounds. He had chosen a fine scene and a little way from him I stopped and got out of my pocket my own small camera to take an instantaneous exposure. As I did so the old gentleman popped out from beneath the dark cloth and I heard a single word in which was such an expression of withering contempt that I have never forgotten it. It was simply " Snapshotter ! " Next moment he had removed the cap from the lens of his camera, made two or three mystic passes with it in the air as though evoking the aid of some deity and replaced it in the manner of one who has performed a religious rite of appalling significance.

Now I am quite certain that the old gentleman grossly over-exposed his plate, for the scene was brilliant and the lighting superlatively good. As for my miserable snap, to me at least it turned out to be a perfectly good photograph revealing the mountain scene accurately and I hope reasonably artistically. And this brings me to the next point—artistry in photography.

At first sight it seems a hopeless task to squeeze a noble mountain several thousands of feet high into the humble dimensions of a film, and a primary mistake in mountain photography is to include too much. It is always better to suggest than to reveal in photography. Anyone seeing a mountain for the first time will be so impressed with its beauty and grandeur that it will not occur to him that height, size and colour when reduced to a small photograph suffer greatly in quality. It is here that the painter scores over the photographer, because he is better able to interpret and reveal by ignoring the unessentials and concentrating on the essentials of the scene. The photographer cannot do this, but he can do a great deal by skilfully arranging the details and lighting of his subject. Yet he must always remember that he cannot vie with the painter and should assume at the outset that photography cannot compete with painting, quite apart from the question of colour.[1] It is a blunder therefore to attempt too much, and the odds are that the photographer who, confronted by one of Nature's grandest scenes, merely points his camera and photographs it will be woefully disappointed with the result. This applies particularly to mountain photography.

[1] For this reason I am opposed to elaborate retouching of the kind so often seen at exhibitions of photographs. I believe that the photographer should make the best of his art and not trespass on another art. Retouching—faking is more brutal but more descriptive—is at its best a bastard art—at its worst it is horrible. No photograph in this book is retouched other than in the removal of mechanical defects in the films or plates such as scratches and pinholes.

2

It is for the above reasons that I would stress the importance of concentrating on suggestion, for the more a photograph suggests beauty, the more beautiful it is as a photograph. One secret of suggestion is composition, and, because the photographer is more limited in his treatment of his subject than is the painter, composition is even more important in photography than it is in painting.

Some there are with a heaven-sent eye for composition and some who can never acquire the rudiments, but there are few who will not benefit from study of this all-important side of photography. Even though they have not a grain of artistic sense in their own composition much can be derived from a rule of thumb application. Everyone who sells a camera should supply gratis a booklet on the principles of composition. There are numerous books on the subject and I would go so far as to say that one or other of these should be studied before purchasing a camera and before anything else is read about the technique of photography, for it is quite certain that ignorance can only result in ugly pictures, and it is surely worth while to bring back a beautiful as well as an interesting record of a holiday on the hills. Much can be learned by visiting art galleries, for the principles underlying composition in painting are precisely similar to those in photography.

The most important thing in landscape photography is the foreground. Even a mountain as intrinsically beautiful as the Matterhorn photographs badly unless accompanied by some sort of foreground. The foreground is the bridge between the eye and the background which in a mountain photograph is usually the theme of the picture. In the absence of any such bridge the eye cannot grasp the scale, whilst the principal details of the photograph lie in a single monotonous plane. Having decided upon something in the foreground, whether it be a tree, a crevasse, a boulder or a human figure, the next thing is to balance it with the background. Parallel lines are to be avoided at all costs, and the principal foreground object should never be directly in line with the principal background object. This simply means that the picture must not be divided into obvious compartments. To have a pine tree geometrically intersecting a distant mountain peak is a fatal mistake; place it a little to one side and the result is a picture. Neither must the foreground clog up the background; it must so balance it that the eye is led willingly not reluctantly forwards. Again, the foreground must

3

never be out of focus or be in focus at the expense of the background ; this is one of the commonest mistakes in photography, and it can be avoided either by stopping down the lens and thereby increasing the depth of focus, which means a longer exposure, or by standing farther away from the foreground object and afterwards trimming the picture— something the mountain photographer will often have to do where he has had no time or facilities for a time exposure. At the same time it is seldom wise to include a foreground simply because there must be one ; however important the main theme, it should be remembered that the foreground is just as important, and indeed I would advocate that the photographer in selecting his foreground takes even more trouble over it than his background.

The final arrangement of the composition depends on the lines of the subject. Nature dislikes straight lines ; the very Earth on which we dwell has a curved surface. She aims at harmony and symmetry : her forms are rhythmical and flowing in their construction, in their sum gentle not brutal. Is it not just, therefore, to portray a mere section of scenery in such a way as to give a false idea of the whole ; rather it should enter into and convey the spirit of the whole. Nowhere in Nature is form more gracious and lines more generous than in mountainous country ; even a supple ash tree or the bold curve of a great river cannot rival the lift of a great hillside towards the clouds. What is there to equal the smooth downward bending surface of a snowfield hemmed about by a whispering gallery of giant crags ? Here are stages set for the time-less dramas of sun and cloud, the delight and despair of all who would record a fragment of their beauty on a piece of celluloid. Consider carefully, then, how these mighty forms and expanses may be most artfully recorded. Look upon each photograph as something containing the subtle ingredients of beauty and consider these carefully before venturing on the fateful and often fatal click of the shutter. Arrange your ingredients nobly ; do not crush them up into a niggardly mess in a single corner or jam them together in a hopeless conglomeration of warring elements. Which is better : a bed of flowers running riot in clashing colours or a single flower ? Simplicity is the soul of Nature and it is the soul of a good photograph. A great multitude of hills widespread to remote horizons may charm the eye—there is witchery in space and distance—but cram them into a film and ugliness is often the

4

result ; a meaningless set of forms hulked one on the other in meaningless disorder.

These lines, the foreground meadow and trees, the curving valley beneath, the upward sweeping facets of the peaks must be arranged. No rule of thumb will do here, no technique of focus and exposure will prevent disaster. There must be some conscious or it may be unconscious artistry in the best photographic work, but much can be gained by studying the principles governing composition. Arrange the picture in the viewfinder as carefully as you would plant a garden. See that the eye passes out of it anxious for more. The meadow, the valley and the hillsides form lines which meet. There may be half a dozen or more of these meeting points or perhaps only one or two in the simplest picture. These meeting points are the focal points of interest. Keep one or two out of the picture and the imagination is stimulated, but keep all of them in view and the picture becomes complicated and complication in a photograph is only another word for dullness.

A picture must balance horizontally and vertically. Therefore try to imagine some pictorial scales. Nature detests sudden jumps ; her progression is rhythmical, yet if you capture a small part of her on a film you may convey an impression of an hiatus which does not in fact exist because the human eye can see farther and assimilate things which the camera cannot because of its limited field of view. Thus, a single black shadow may pass unnoticed by the eye but it becomes very noticeable when it fills a large portion of a photograph. In mountain photography we pot nature, and to make our dish palatable we must include not only the correct number of ingredients but the correct proportion.

Lighting, though it must be studied separately, is yet an integral part of composition inasmuch as it accentuates or represses the lines and details of a photograph. Poor lighting cannot make the finest lineal composition effective. Perhaps the most pernicious advice ever ladled out to the beginner in photography is " keep the sun behind your back." The fact is that the majority of effective landscape and mountain photographs are taken with the sun somewhere in the half circle in front of the photographer, and many instances justify a photograph directly into the sun provided that the lens be shielded or clouds conceal or diffuse the sun. Snow scenes are particularly effective taken in this way as the texture of the snow is revealed and the photograph becomes full of subtle incident. The most dreary and inartistic pictures of snow scenes are those taken with the sun shining from directly behind the photographer. Such photographs are either flat in tone or harsh with a soot and whitewash effect, the rocks being soot and the snow whitewash. Study of the great majority of photographs in this book will reveal a sun seldom in the arc behind the photographer. The lower the sun the more important it is to arrange the lighting. The shadows become longer, deeper and broader and tend to dominate the picture, and only skilful arranging can produce a balanced picture. The worst hours for mountain photography are from 10 a.m. to 2 p.m., for then the lighting is flattest, though this to some extent depends on the season, good photography being possible all through a winter's day. This of course is a generalisation, as clouds can aid lighting effects at any hour of the day.

A problem the mountain photographer is often up against is whether he shall sacrifice detail in his shadows in order to reveal detail in his high lights, which would otherwise be over-exposed. My experience is that no successful compromise is possible with an ordinary orthochromatic film and that panchromatic film must be used if the finest tone gradations are to be secured. This again is a generalisation; many pictures in this book were taken on orthochromatic film and it is difficult to detect the difference between these and those taken on panchromatic film. However, on the whole panchromatic film not only gives better tone values but avoids the soot and whitewash effect already mentioned which so often results when snow scenes are taken on orthochromatic film. To many beginners the word panchromatic has a sinister ring about it; it is only for skilled photographers, they think. Such is by no means the case nowadays. There are films on the market which allow great latitude of exposure so that a beginner, even though he be unprovided with an exposure meter should be able to secure good photographs. I use " Panatomic " film and have found it the best of many I have tried on the hills.

Filters are often a vexed problem, and it may be of interest to state that only about one in five of the pictures in this book were taken through them. Many photographers striving after effect use dense filters which result in over corrected landscapes and dark skies against which clouds stand out in vivid relief. There is no doubt that the judicious use of a filter can improve many pictures and it is almost

6

essential when photographing scenes which combine grass, forest and snow mountains, and in correcting what would otherwise appear too contrasty. Grass in combination with a snow mountain provides too great a tone difference for the film and will print too darkly, whilst the snow will be too featureless and not stand out boldly against the sky unless a filter is used. What density of filter to use is a matter of experience. I use green, yellow and red, obtaining more dramatic pictures through the last colour. Whether or not fidelity of tone is to be aimed at when reproducing a mountain scene is a matter of opinion. Many will have been struck by the unnaturally dark appearance of the sky in the earlier photographs of Mount Everest. Some fine photographs were taken by the first expedition but many appear as though they were taken by flashlight, the mountains being grim and ghostly against an almost black sky in which clouds stand out with brutal distinctness. Whether or not you like these pictures is again a matter of opinion. I do not, because having seen the original scenes I know them to be unnatural. This unnatural and dramatic quality is carried a stage further by the infra-red plate which to my mind produces pictures which are interesting without being beautiful. The sky at high altitudes even in the Alps is a darker blue than at sea level owing to the moisture-free air, but it is by no means black. Is it not better to regard photography as a means of reproducing nature as faithfully as possible ? On high snow peaks whether they be in the Alps or the Himalayas faithful pictures can be secured without a filter, or at the most a very light filter, say one merely doubling the exposure. Denser filters may be used for denser atmospheres or as already suggested for valley scenes where heavy tones are undesirable or when far horizons are to be included.

In the past, exposure was a fruitful source of failure, but modern films allow a wide latitude and modern exposure meters are so accurate that the veriest novice need no longer fear the bogey. At the same time, it must be remembered that every scene worth photographing deserves to be rendered with the utmost fidelity and this can only be obtained when the exposure is accurate, there being a world of difference between a good and a perfect photograph. This is where the miniature camera scores, taking pictures on 35 mm. film, as in cases of doubt it is easy to take two or three pictures of the same subject giving each a different exposure.

7

Exposure meters are legion, but there is little doubt that the photo-electric principle is the best, though it must be remembered that it becomes inaccurate when used at high altitudes owing to the increased amount of ultra-violet light in the atmosphere. I must confess that I do not use an exposure meter and none of the photographs in this book were taken with the aid of one ; this is no claim to skill, but a confession of laziness ; albums of my total failures would fill several bookshelves.

It is perhaps unwise to talk about perfectly exposed pictures as opinions differ as to what is a perfectly exposed picture. In mountain photography I prefer to aim for brilliant rather than dense negatives —negatives on the thin side which have plenty of detail in both shadows and high lights. I believe that better results are to be obtained by printing a thin negative on to a fastish paper than by printing a dense negative on to slow paper, though I expect those more expert than I will disagree violently here.

In mountain photography it is seldom necessary to take a time-exposure unless dense filters are used. Exposures in mountainous countries are difficult to gauge. For instance, in the lower valleys of the Himalayas it is essential to give a far greater exposure than seems necessary, whilst the exact reverse applies at high altitudes. The same is true of Switzerland though the difference is not so marked. Light plays queer pranks ; why is it that a man can go hatless up the Amazon without danger of sunstroke, and not do so in Northern India which is outside the tropics ?

Apparatus is largely a matter of personal taste. It may be assumed that the camera for mountain photography should be light and portable and small enough to be carried in the pocket as it is an annoying business to have to extract it from a rucksack, especially on a difficult climb ; the photographer can be as much a nuisance as a blessing to an expedition. I have tried various cameras, but the best I have yet discovered for mountain photography is the " Etui." This will take either film packs or plates, but as there are few who want to be bothered with the latter, especially as film packs are nowadays so reliable, it is a good idea to have the film pack adapter fastened permanently to the back of the camera as this prevents fogging of the film as well as the tedious necessity to use a dark slide which, as I know from bitter experience, is easily forgotten in the heat of the moment. The best all-round size is a $2\frac{1}{2}$ inches by

8

$3\frac{1}{2}$ inches film, as with modern almost grainless films of this size enlargements up to or exceeding 25 inches by 30 inches can be made. The "Etui" in this size weighs only one pound and one film pack of twelve negatives adds four ounces. Many, however, prefer the miniature cameras such as the "Leica" and the "Retina"—indeed miniature cameras, by reason of the three dozen pictures they can take on one spool of film, and the low cost of photography, are the vogue. It should be remembered, however, that enlargements much over 10 or 12 inches are unsatisfactory as compared with those from a larger negative and for this reason I favour the $2\frac{1}{2}$ inches by $3\frac{1}{2}$ inches camera. Furthermore, most of the miniature cameras weigh more than the "Etui" which despite its lightness and portability is very strong and durable.

The mountain photographer seldom needs a shutter speed in excess of 1/50 of a second, and there is no object in having an elaborate shutter as this merely adds to the weight. A great many cameras are nowadays fitted with the "Compur" shutter and this is very reliable except under conditions of extreme cold when there is sometimes a noticeable slowing down of its speed, a point which need not concern Alpine mountaineers. Perhaps the simplest and most reliable shutter for mountain work is a self-setting shutter actuated by a strong spring as there is no complicated mechanism to go wrong.

One gadget I have found to be indispensable is the delay action which is fitted to many "Compur" shutters. This gives a 15 seconds delay after the shutter mechanism has been set in motion so that the photographer may include himself in the picture which is often desirable where a human figure is necessary to set off the scale of the subject or to add life and foreground to a picture; incidentally not nearly enough mountain pictures are taken in which human figures play their part, though it is unfortunately only too easy to mar a picture by interposing someone unskilfully posed.

Except for photographs of topographical interest a wide angle lens is thoroughly unsatisfactory and when taking mountain photographs I have always favoured a lens of slightly longer focus than the standard lens supplied in most cameras. Generally speaking, the more a mountain photograph includes the less effective it is and, as already pointed out, it should be the aim of the photographer to concentrate on one particular aspect of a mountain landscape rather than try to include as much as possible. For this reason a long rather than a short focus lens is indispensable. Telephoto lenses are simply extra long focus lenses which include so small a portion of the subject that some form of support is necessary for the camera both for focussing and exposure, which is necessarily greater than that with a short focus lens. A telephoto lens is a most desirable adjunct as, apart from the interesting subjects which may be obtained and for topographical purposes, it can by seizing on one small portion of a mountain scene make an effective picture where none is possible otherwise. It must be conceded, however, that from an artistic standpoint the difficulty of foreground is not easily overcome, and considerably more skill is necessary in taking effective telephotographs than in taking ordinary photographs. Generally speaking, the principal subject must itself be effective enough to allow of a foreground being dispensed with.

The mountaineer will need something better than a mere contact print to remind him of his holiday. No finer record is obtainable than by having enlargements made in the carbon or carbro processes, both of which possess the advantage of permanency. The carbon process necessitates making an enlarged negative and is therefore expensive compared with the bromide process if only one or two enlargements are required; in the case of several copies, however, it is cheaper. In no photographic subject does an enlargement bring out beauty and grandeur better than in a mountain photograph, for every lineal inch makes the scale more apparent. In this connection there is little doubt that one really magnificent enlargement is worth a host of small ones, and the photographer thinking of decorating his walls will do well to concentrate on but a few of his best pictures. A fine enlargement of a mountain scene equips thought with swift wings and enables the mountaineer to live through once again a glorious day on the mountains.

THE BRITISH HILLS

THE British hills culminate in the summit of Ben Nevis, but it is not so easy to say where they begin. Have the Downs a right to be included in a book on mountain photography? If so, why not Constitution Hill? Some sort of a definition is needed and most people would agree that the essential attribute of a hill is that it should be wild and unspoilt by the hand of man. If this be so then there are many hills in Britain ranging from the pines and heather of Holmbury Hill, where it is quite easy to lose yourself on a misty day, to the lonelier and grander hills of the Lake District, Wales and Scotland, not to mention the western moors and the desolate sweeps of the Pennines.

In spite of those unprincipled vandals who seek to capitalise our most cherished scenery and, what is almost worse, those misguided people who seek to " improve " it by afforestation on slopes where we and our ancestors have been accustomed to see nothing but rocks, heather and the mighty gathering of lights and shadows, there is still much left to us and for those who come after us. Perhaps there may be more in the future, thanks to the mercifully falling birth rate. To those who measure the dignity of men or mountains by lineal inches, the British hills are unworthy of serious attention, but to those who have learnt their secrets, who have walked and climbed over them at all seasons and in all weathers, who have first balanced themselves on a tiny hold, or back-and-kneed up a vertical chimney, they are infinitely precious. And the more the mountaineer explores the remoter ranges of the world, the higher he climbs, the more joyfully he returns to the rocks and heather of these hills, and the more he learns that height is no measure of beauty, or even of grandeur.

II. ON HOLMBURY HILL

It is not inappropriate that a volume of mountain photographs should begin with a photograph taken within a few miles of London on a gentle ridge of the North Downs, even though it includes photographs taken at the greatest elevations so far attained in the world, for most British mountaineers have graduated in the British hills and there must be many whose love of the hills dates from week-end strolls over the Downs. The mountaineer home from the greater ranges is often asked whether he does not find the British hills insignificant. The answer is that the beauty and majesty of the hills is not translatable in terms of mere height. It is no anticlimax to return from Everest to Holmbury Hill; on the contrary, the gracious contours of the English countryside have a charm so distinct that comparisons are as futile as they are ridiculous. So far as my own experience goes there is no countryside so beautiful as the English countryside and no hills so carefree as the English hills.

II

III

III. DERWENTWATER

The English Lake District is small, little more than twenty miles square, but it is very precious and the brightest jewel in the crown of English scenery. Efforts are being made to preserve it so that future generations may enjoy its beauties, and large tracts have become national property. There is no hill district abounding in such rich and varied yet soft and delicate colourings, none where the horizons are so far and dim or the peace more profound. Yet, but a few miles away, factory chimneys pour their smoke over gaunt landscapes.

To the photographer the reproduction of one tithe of this beauty is a supremely difficult task. I am ashamed to think of the plates and films I have wasted, how the soft blue hills ranked one behind the other have defied the camera and been transmuted with all their marvellous tones and colours into grey lifeless outlines. Good lighting there must be—it is useless trying to capture the mournful sublimity of these hills when the wet mists from the Atlantic cling to them. Foreground is more essential here than anywhere. Only through contrast is distance percept- ible and distance is the keynote of the British hills. Choose your foreground even more carefully than your background.

IV. SUNSET FROM BEN NEVIS

The Scottish hills are colourful and mysterious in the long June evenings. All through the night the north sky is filled with light and the delicate blues, purples, greens and golds are the inspiration and the despair of the photographer. It is an unforgettable experience to emerge on to the summit plateau of Ben Nevis into the westering sun from one of the ridges or gullies of the steep, dark northern side of the mountain. When this photograph was taken the hour was late but the sun was still well above the horizon and its rays were reflected by Loch Linnhe stretching south-westwards into the Atlantic haze.

V. THE SUMMIT OF LLIWEDD

Lliwedd is the highest crag in England and Wales and the finest of the Welsh climbing grounds. Its dark cliffs rising in a bold sweep from the darker waters of Llyn Llydaw are a familiar sight to all visitors to the Snowdon district. In this photograph a climb has just been completed and the climbers have been rewarded with a view such as is only possible in the British hills—a glimpse through a misty luminous atmosphere across blue hills chequered with light and shadow. Here is an example where the interposition of a human figure adds to the interest of a photograph as it helps to carry the eye onwards and outwards. The fact that he is obviously intent on regarding the view adds a dramatic quality to the photograph as well as relieving it from a certain monotony.

16

IV

V

VI

VII

VI. A HIGHLAND BURN

Running water imparts life into any landscape and the hill stream often relieves a photograph of the British hills of that element of drab monotony which is often so difficult to avoid where colour, vastness and subtle tone gradations must all be brought into the compass of a small black and white film or plate. Furthermore, the curve of a stream as it winds its way sinuously through the heather can be harmonised with the long lift of a distant hill so that through careful composition of the main lines the photographer is often able to extract the prime elements of beauty from the most unpromising material.

VII. LOOKING SOUTHWARDS FROM BEN LAWERS

Ben Lawers is a hill 3,984 feet high to the north-west of Loch Tay in Perthshire in the Southern Highlands. The photograph was taken after an early winter snowfall which had covered the ground above the 2,000 feet level. I have long come to the conclusion that the Highlands of Scotland are the most difficult of all hills to photograph effectively. The lighting is not easy to gauge owing to the low angle of the sun during the winter months and more particularly because of the amount of water vapour usually present in the air, whilst the absence of trees adds to the difficulty of selecting a foreground which will aid the eye to appreciate the scale—a difficulty which applies to all the higher British hills. Thus the photographer must depend on the direction and angle of hillsides and ridges when composing his picture. Clouds and cloud shadows are a standby, for both enhance the apparent distance which is so hard to render effectively in hill photographs. The accompanying photograph is a case in point, though not by any means a good one.

19

THE EASTERN ALPS

THE Eastern Alps cannot boast mountains to compare in height and the length of their difficulties with those of the Swiss and the French Alps, yet in beauty and charm they are not surpassed anywhere. Here is an ideal country for all who delight in hill wandering, and the excellent huts, really mountain hotels, of the German and Austrian Alpine Club make possible many long and high tours with the minimum of food and equipment, though it must be remembered that these mountains are as capable of severe and dangerous weather as the greater Alps.

Although visited by many thousands of tourists, most of the Tyrolese villages and valleys retain their simple charm and the traveller is still made to feel that he is welcome at the inns and that the depth of his pocket is not the only consideration. To the photographer Tyrol is a paradise, for there is every combination that the pictorialist can desire in its fertile valleys with their flower-clad meadows and quaint villages, its torrents, forests and snow-clad peaks. Many of my happiest mountain days have been spent rambling, scrambling and climbing in this country, and a camera has usually accompanied me.

For the sake of convenience the Engadine and the Alps of Glarus have been included in this section. The former, particularly the Bernina and Bregaglia, provide splendid mountaineering, though the routes are somewhat shorter than those on the higher peaks of the Pennines, the Oberland and the range of Mont Blanc. The latter are little visited by British mountaineers but are nevertheless charming and include within a few square miles some of the most formidable precipices and beautiful valleys in the Alps. There are few more impressive gorges than that at the head of the Linthal or valleys more flowerful than the Maderanerthal. I owe an apology to the reader for not including the Dolomites and the Ortler group. I have climbed on the former but not on the latter. Such photographs as I have do not begin to do justice to a country unique in its beauty. The Dolomites resemble a parkland of the gods rather than a conventional mountain range, and I would prefer

20

to revisit them and re-photograph them before attempting to reveal their extraordinary peaks to the critical reader. It seems to me, looking back on my total failure to photograph them effectively—I was a complete novice at photography sixteen years ago—that panchromatic films or plates and a dense filter, perhaps a red one, are necessary to reveal their reds and yellows in combination with the bright green pastures that surround them. I may be wrong and the experiences of others would be interesting.

VIII. WINTER MORNING NEAR ST. ANTON

A few years ago St. Anton-am-Arlberg was almost unknown to winter sportsmen, but it is now one of the most popular ski-ing centres in the Alps. This is due to splendid ski-ing country and the famous Arlberg ski-ing school founded after the war by Hannes Schneider. In my student days I was fortunate enough to spend a whole winter there and make scores of ski-ing expeditions on the neighbouring peaks. Owing to my ignorance of photography few of the photographs I took during this period do any justice to the scenery of the district which, if not comparable in grandeur to the Swiss Alps, has a charm all its own owing to its long wooded valleys leading upwards to vast snowfields where many long ski runs are possible. This is perhaps a conventional composition with a snow-laden branch in the foreground, chalets in the middle distance and a peak in the background, yet it serves to demonstrate one or two basic principles in photography of which the most important are simplicity of arrangement as well as the diffusion and balance of the main details so that the eye is reposed rather than stimulated into restlessness. Lastly, the lighting was so arranged that the sun was well in front of the camera.

VIII

IX

IX. PINE RANKS: ST. ANTON

A pine forest laden with freshly fallen snow always makes an attractive subject for the camera, principally because snow reveals the beauty of the trees which are otherwise somewhat dull and unattractive when photographed collectively. Yet, in order to suggest the simple yet beautifully massed ranks of the forest, contrast is essential, and this is best gained through the medium of a path or river as this immediately suggests distance by leading the eye forwards without conscious effort. Such photographs also suggest the intense stillness and silence of the Alps in winter when the streams are frozen and frost lays its hand on every living thing. This silence is one of the most wonderful aspects of the mountains and it is all the more evident to people used to spending the greater part of their lives amid noise. It is a silence which can be *felt*. In the still frosty air, when there is not a single breath of wind to send the feathery crystals of snow pouring like salt from the branches, the ear strains itself but discovers only silence— a silence charged with the vital forces of the Universe, visible and invisible.

X. A FROZEN STREAM

One brilliant morning I was out ski-ing on the Arlberg hills near St. Anton when I chanced upon a frozen stream covered in frost flowers. It was a beautiful subject but difficult to photograph effectively. A piece representative of the whole had to be selected, and this is always a tricky matter in photography, though it is a basic principle in landscape work. Background and foreground had to blend peacefully whilst lighting was of supreme importance. I believe I spent half an hour composing the picture. The frost flowers serve to break up an otherwise unimportant foreground, whilst the shadows in the snow and the dark belt of pine forest heighten the brilliant high lights where the sun, directly in line with the lens but well above it, is reflected from the ice. Perhaps the principal feature is the format of the gently curving yet bold lines whose points of intersection are well outside the picture. Such lines stimulate the imagination without jarring on the pictorial sense. Harsh, brutally intersecting lines must be avoided at all costs in pictorial photography.

X

XI

XII

XI. THE KRIMML FALLS

At the western end of the Pinzgau Tal is the village of Krimml, easily accessible by narrow gauge railway from Zell-am-See, and above it are the famous Krimml Falls, reputed the finest in the Alps, if not in Europe, where the glacier waters of the Krimmler Bach descend over a series of crags totalling several hundred feet in height. To photograph them is much like photographing any other waterfall—largely a matter of luck and lighting. This photograph was taken on a misty rainy day when the sun was trying to edge through the clouds, circumstances which combined to make an effective picture—if a trifle under-exposed. The principal difficulty was arranging the pine trees to form an appropriate framework as there is no photographic subject where a foreground is more necessary than a waterfall. Exposure when photographing rapidly moving water should never be less than 1/50 of a second, otherwise the water will appear unnaturally smooth and blurred, a fault often noticeable in otherwise excellent pictures.

XII. THE OBER-SULZBACH TAL

Tumbling waters are always a pleasant subject to photograph and when in addition these have as their setting dark pine forests and silver-lit snow the picture is complete. The Ober-Sulzbach Tal in the Hohe Tauern is typical of many delightful valleys in the Austrian Alps ; there are pine forests, fertile alps with abundant flowers, a glacier system and some high peaks at the end of it and a tumultuous torrent of glacier water, hastening to join the Danube. Such pictures readily compose themselves provided no attempt is made to mix into them too many ingredients.

XIII. THE SUMMIT OF THE WILDGERLOS SPITZE

The Reichen range stands a little apart from the Hohe Tauern and the Zillertal ranges. Its highest peaks only just exceed 11,000 feet, but it is interesting and charming and some first-rate scrambling is to be had there. Campbell Secord and I spent a happy day traversing several of the principal peaks and this photograph was taken on the last summit we visited. It was late in the afternoon and the rocks were warm with the accumulated heat of the sun; there was not a breath of wind and the ridges of the Bavarian Alps in the north-east were outlined by bands of purple haze which filled the valleys like a fluid to a certain level. While my companion stood on the sharp upturned slabs of the summit I retreated a few yards and photographed him and the view. It would be a dull even monotonous picture were it not for the belts of haze which by separating the distant ridges give an impression of distance and to a lesser extent depth. Furthermore, my companion is nicely poised—it is fatally easy to spoil a picture by interposing a human figure especially one looking the wrong way—whilst the sharp, clean jointed slabs bite savagely and effectively into the luminous background.

XIII

XIV

XIV. THE NORTH-WEST RIDGE OF THE GROSS VENEDIGER

Mountain ridges viewed end on are always difficult to photograph as the camera no less than the eye is deceived by foreshortening and the main features of a ridge, its towers and gaps, are jumbled together. The photographer must seize the rare opportunities when they occur of a comprehensive view along the crest. The north-west ridge of the Gross Venediger is the finest as well as the most difficult ridge of a peak which, by the ordinary route, is nothing but a snow walk. It was the last climb Campbell Secord and I made when we traversed the Austrian Alps, and the photograph conveys some idea of a fine sweeping edge artfully broken up into rocky towers separated by blades of snow and ice. The principal merit of such a photograph is that it is able to reveal just sufficient of the ridge to prolong the upward passage of the eye, and thereby impress it with a sense of height and distance in spite of inevitable foreshortening, whilst the sharp parabolic snow edges suggest the keenest of all delights in mountaineering, that of treading a virgin snow ridge leading to the summit of a peak.

XV. THE SAMNAUN TAL

The Samnaun Tal is one of the most easterly Swiss valleys and is well away from tourist routes, though an excellent road connects it with the Inn Tal and the Unter Engadine. If it does not possess the dramatic qualities of the better-known Swiss valleys it is very beautiful, particularly in its middlemost and uppermost portions, and in spring and early summer countless flowers bloom. Valley photography is not easy in the absence of a dramatic foreground or background and in this picture I have tried to convey quiet charm through the medium of delicate tone gradation, in which the camera has been greatly helped by a series of descending slopes and ridges, whilst a small outjutting crag embowered with creamy anemones forms a necessary foreground to set off both height and distance. Panchromatic film is essential, otherwise only the most brilliant lighting will relieve the photograph from dullness and such lighting in this instance was inimical to a picture which depends on softness rather than boldness of tone for its effect.

34

XV

XVI

XVI. DAWN ON THE ROSEG GLACIER

On three occasions in midwinter I have set off from the Cöaz Hut to climb the Piz Roseg, but each time was foiled by bad weather to which the high peaks of the Engadine would appear to be peculiarly susceptible at this season. This photograph was taken after a friend and I had been confined to the hut for three days by a blizzard. A stormy dawn greeted us on the Roseg glacier and it was apparent that we should fail to achieve our objective. However, I managed to bring back a record of the occasion to remind me of the splendour of the prospect : my companion in the foreground slowly ploughing through soft, deep " Pulverschnee," his curving track leading the eye onwards across the glacier, and a distant range of peaks over which the sun is struggling feebly through gathering stormclouds. The photograph was carefully planned so that no harsh dominating line should cleave it and the balance carefully preserved between the curving ski track and the background of peaks, clouds and sunlight. A short exposure and a thin but brilliant negative with plenty of detail are the secrets of successful dawn and sunset pictures.

XVII. THE MADERANER TAL FROM THE HÜFI HUT

In 1934 during a solitary traverse of Switzerland on ski I crossed the Clariden Pass from Linthal to Amsteg. In descending from the pass I was overtaken by the Föhn wind and was fortunate to reach the Hüfi hut safely after traversing some very dangerous snow slopes. This hut is situated on a projecting spur overlooking the Maderaner Tal, the floor of which is fully 4,000 feet below. All through the afternoon after I had reached the hut great avalanches roared and smoked down the steep slopes into the valley, but towards evening the moisture-laden clouds began to break up and this photograph was one of several taken at that period. Depth, always difficult to convey in a photograph, is perhaps suggested by the interposition of an outjutting snow-covered crag in the foreground which serves as a foil to the valley stream 4,000 feet lower. Brilliancy in such photographs is only achieved through a short exposure with a small stop, and the small negative from which this picture was made errs if anything on the side of thinness.

XVII

XVIII

XIX

XVIII–XIX. CROCUSES ON THE FELLI ALP

One spring morning in 1934 I climbed through a steep pine forest above Amsteg bound for the Felli Lücke, a pass I was crossing en route to Andermatt. After a toilsome ascent I emerged on to an alp. As I left the gloom of the forest I had almost to rub my eyes. Had I come unexpectedly to snow? No, not snow, but crocuses, the bravest display of these flowers I have ever seen. The slopes of a secluded little alp were ablaze; there were avenues of bloom between the boulders; a celestial carpet was laid over the damp turf. The upright photograph is under-exposed a trifle; the horizontal photograph is better exposed. Both are simple pictures though I feel that the composition in the horizontal one at least could have been improved upon, yet the glory of the scene almost defied carefully calculated composition; it seemed enough to point the camera and trust that it would faithfully record it.

THE BERNESE OBERLAND

THE Bernese Oberland has one great advantage from a mountaineering standpoint over the Pennine Alps or the range of Mont Blanc—the mountaineer may cross any of its passes or peaks without being shot at or cast into an Italian dungeon. For the rest there is no Alpine range which offers such a diversity of scenery within a short horizontal distance. This last is apparent when approaching it from the north and many who read this will remember the turn in the railway line near Thun which brings into view the Jungfrau, Mönch and Eiger. The names given to the peaks reveal the feeling of the peasantry towards summits that have looked down on their small affairs through many centuries of change and evolution: The Maiden (Jungfrau) the Monk (Mönch), the Ogre (Eiger), the Peak of Storms (Wetterhorn), the Peak of Terror (Schreckhorn) and the Field of Eternal Snow (Ewig Schneefeld).

From a mountaineering standpoint the Oberland is essentially a region of first rate snow- and ice-peaks, and this fact is borne out by the excellence of the guides in snow- and ice-craft. Broadly speaking, it is said that the Grindelwald guides are snow- and ice-men, the Chamonix guides expert on rocks and the Zermatt and St. Niklaus guides all-round mountaineers. Of late the Oberland guides have had to test their metal not on snow and ice but on the north face of the Eiger which since the ascent of the north faces of the Matterhorn and the Grandes Jorasses has attracted numerous young Germans and Austrians of the do-or-die school. It has been their unenviable task to succour the stricken and recover the remains of the fallen.

The one disadvantage of the Oberland is the weather, for this district by reason of its proximity to the warm Rhone Valley has an evil reputation for bad weather. The worst storm I was ever in occurred with little warning on the Schreckhorn, and I have experienced two weeks of Föhn wind without a break. Yet, admitting its disadvantages,

42

there is no district possessing a more distinctive charm. Exactly what this charm is it is hard to say. Is it because the mountaineer can look down on green hills and pasture? Or is it because when he treads the inner sanctuaries of the snows he feels completely cut off from all life and can see naught but wastes of rock and ice?

XX. THE EIGER FROM THE SCHRECKHORN

Nothing helps the eye to appreciate the height of a mountain better than belts of cloud ; indeed the ever-changing vistas clouds afford render the smallest mountain range inexhaustible from a photographer's standpoint. The Eiger throws down its steepest and finest side towards Grindelwald and the Kleine Scheidegg, but it is almost equally fine when viewed from the south. The former side has recently acquired an unenviable notoriety owing to the desperate attempts by young Germans and Austrians to climb it. Several lives have been lost from among the ranks of these " storm troopers " and the Grindelwald guides have had to engage on rescue expeditions little less desperate in succour of those overtaken by bad weather and powerless to retreat down the precipice. As a result of these wholly unjustifiable attempts the Swiss government placed a ban on the precipice—an unwise move as it only added to its notoriety— whilst one authority suggested that intending suicides should provide in advance the wherewithal for their own search parties and funeral expenses. The south face of the mountain seen in this photograph is also still unclimbed and will doubtless take its toll of life before it is " conquered " ; it is desperately dangerous on account of falling stones, and consists of smooth-looking indeterminate limestone slabs of such a ferocious nature as to daunt the most ardent searcher after the " impossible."

XX

XXI

XXII

XXI. STORM CLOUDS ON THE FINSTERAARHORN

In July 1925 J. H. B. Bell and I left the Concordia Hut with the intention of crossing the Agassizjoch which lies between the Agassizhorn and the Finsteraarhorn. The dawn sky was, however, so threatening that we decided to abandon our climb and make for the Finsteraarhorn Hut. We had barely reached the hut—within an hour after this photograph was taken—when there broke a thunderstorm and blizzard of exceptional violence. Another party on the Jungfrau were not so lucky as we and one of its members died in the storm. It is noteworthy that the dawn was accompanied by a curious green glow which pervaded the atmosphere. The photograph which gives some idea of the ominous sky was taken from the Grünhorn Lücke.

XXII. THE FIESCHERHÖRNER

Were it not for the clouds and shaft of sunlight this photograph would be thoroughly bad and uninteresting, for there is no foreground to direct the eye and the main object, the Fiescherhörner, appears as an irregular ridge of peaks with little to recommend it from a picture-making standpoint. The interplay of light and cloud, however, makes all the difference. It is seldom that the photographer has the time to wait for exactly the right arrangement of light and cloud, but on this occasion there was no hurry and I remained an hour seated on a boulder near the Strahlegg Pass until a shaft of sunlight penetrated the mists to fall obliquely on a beautifully moulded snow ridge.

XXIII. THE AGASSIZHORN

The Agassizhorn was named after the noted Swiss naturalist and is a peak on a ridge extending northwards from the Finsteraarhorn in the Bernese Oberland. Like its greater neighbour, it falls steeply to the east, and the photograph, taken during an ascent of the Klein Fiescherhorn, gives a fair idea of this face. I was fortunate when taking it inasmuch as the lighting was perfect, the sun being still two or three hours from its zenith, an important point as Alpine photographs taken at midday are seldom so effective as those before 10 a.m. and after 2 p.m. Thus, the sun was shining obliquely downwards from a point almost directly in front of the camera and was reflected brilliantly from the ice slopes but not too brilliantly so as to destroy all detail in the high lights. The picture may be said to compose itself except that care was needed to relieve a somewhat featureless foreground from monotony by choosing a point where the slope was broken. For the rest, the sublime sweep of the peak lifting into the deep blue sky is dramatic enough in itself to delight the eye, and the photograph was simply a matter of luck.

XXIII

XXIV

XXIV. THE FIESCHERWAND

Certain subjects lend themselves to long panel-like photographs, and this picture of the Fiescherwand above Grindelwald is a case in point. It was obtained with a $4\frac{1}{4}$ by $2\frac{1}{2}$ inches camera, but similar results are possible by trimming a squarer negative or print ; indeed the photographer should never allow the scissors or trimming knife out of his reach. An analysis of this photograph discloses three main points in its composition ; the delicate tracery of ice ribs and avalanche-worn channels leading the eye downwards and upwards, the *Bergschrund* cleaving across them at the foot of the slope and the dark cliff and sweeping ridge in the background capped with a line of cloud emphasising its height and remoteness. Another important fact is that the sun was shining almost directly into the lens. This adds greatly to the effectiveness of the picture by interposing a high light between the camera and the dark background cliff. The Fiescherwand is a fine wall and there are now several routes up it, all very difficult. The most difficult lies up the rock wall in the background and culminates in the summit of the Klein Fiescherhorn.

XXV. ABOVE MÜRREN

A ski track cleaving a snowfield is always an attractive subject to the photographer as the perusal of any ski-ing periodical will prove; indeed it is photographed *ad nauseam* by amateur and professional alike and is the stand-by of innumerable wintersport poster artists. Here is a simple composition; a snow-weighted pine edging into the picture, a ski track tailing away into the distance, a not ungraceful background of gently moulded hillside and a figure to add a touch of life to an otherwise lifeless scene. Adequate lighting is the secret of successful wintersport photography and by this I do not mean merely bright lighting but the illumination of the snow in such a way so as to reveal its texture. Never was such pernicious advice given to the novice in photography as " keep the sun behind you," for snow photographs at least are rarely if ever successful unless the sun occupies one part or other of the semicircle before the photographer. Thin but brilliant negatives full of detail are the other part of the story. Expose as little as you dare in the photography of snow scenes.

XXV

XXVI

XXVII

XXVI. A CREST ON THE BLÜMLISALPHORN

The lofty snows of the Blümlisalp are familiar to visitors to Kandersteg and the western wing of the Bernese Oberland. The Blümlisalphorn, the highest peak in the massif, is not a difficult climb and commands a splendid view of the Pennine Alps to the south and particularly of the Weisshorn which stands out above everything, dominating even the Matterhorn, whose solitary pyramid is discernible to the left of it. To the south, the Blümlisalphorn falls in steep cliffs overhung in many places with cornices. Thus, a photograph looking along the crest is particularly impressive, as these volutes of snow suggest an ocean wave, and an impression of depth is gained even in a horizontal picture without the necessity to reveal it directly.

XXVII. STORMCLOUDS ON THE BIETSCHHORN

The finest peak of the western Oberland is the Bietschhorn which, like many another high and isolated peak, attracts to itself much bad weather. Owing to the steep glaciers surrounding it, it is not an easy mountain to photograph and in this picture it appears considerably foreshortened. The only pictorial merit is the play of light and cloud to which the curving glacier in the foreground adds in some small degree.

THE PENNINE ALPS

THE Pennine Alps extend from the Col Ferret to the Simplon Pass and form the frontier as well as the watershed between Switzerland and Italy. After Mont Blanc the highest and many of the finest Alpine peaks are situated in this section. Highest of all is Monte Rosa, 15,217 feet, of which the Dufour Spitze is the loftiest summit in Switzerland, but the undisputed monarch of the district is the Matterhorn which, despite attempts to vulgarise it and the hordes of trippers who are annually lugged up it by sturdy guides, remains unique among the mountains of the world.

Zermatt is the principal climbing centre but climbers gravitate also to Arolla and Saas Fee. From a purely climbing point of view many climbers will agree that the best the Pennines can offer is not equal to the best routes on the range of Mont Blanc, yet the peaks possess a greater individuality than the subsidiary peaks of Mont Blanc and in this lies their charm ; whether it be the Matterhorn, the Dent Blanche, the Rothhorn, the Weisshorn or many other of the greater Zermatt peaks, the mountaineer has a feeling that he is on a great mountain as distinct from a subsidiary point in a high and concentrated massif of peaks.

From a photographic point of view there are greater and more varied opportunities in the Zermatt district for fine photography than in any Alpine district, though the photographer has always an uncomfortable feeling that every possible angle has been explored by the Swiss professionals whose works adorn the stalls and shop windows in Zermatt and other popular centres. Yet he can take heart in the thought that the mountains exhibit endless combinations of cloud and lighting, and that even in the case of the Matterhorn, a goldmine to vendors of films, no two photographs are likely to be exactly similar.

Owing to good paths and mountain railways the non-mountaineer has an infinitude of subjects at his disposal which combine fertile valleys and flowerful alps with the high snows. A walk up to the Schönbühl Hut will reveal many a fine subject, whilst the ever-changing vistas from the Gornergrat railway invariably set a whole battery of cameras clicking.

56

Time and again the photographer falls under the spell of the Matterhorn; how often the exhibitions at the Alpine Club will reveal. Ever, as he climbs other peaks, he searches for some new angle, some unusual combination of ridges and glaciers as a worthy setting to this extraordinary peak. Yet the Matterhorn is but one peak among many in this district. The Weisshorn, the Rothhorn, the Obergabelhorn, Monte Rosa and a host of other great mountains all tax our ingenuity and skill to reveal them as they should be revealed, not as a gigantic photographic muddle without form or void imprisoned within the relentless limits of a piece of celluloid, but simply. If we remember that simplicity is the soul of photography, and it is the hardest of all things to remember when the temptation is strong upon us to cram as much as possible of a superb panorama into a photograph, we shall do such justice to our subjects as is possible within the limits of photography.

XXVIII. THE MATTERHORN: DAWN

The Matterhorn is a rock peak and at dawn cannot show the ethereal beauties of a snow peak. It resembles some titanic forging alive and glowing at one end, becoming molten as the sunlight strengthens. Even a panchromatic film does scant justice to an Alpine dawn as it leaves colour to the imagination—the dark purples of the night-filled valleys and the glowing heights set in an amethyst sky.

XXIX. MONTE ROSA: EARLY MORNING

The mountaineer starts early, and often the first hour or two of his climb is made by lantern light so that dawn usually finds him in a position to appreciate the beauty of this period. Dawn's first hint in the high mountains is conveyed by a gradual lightening of the upper snows. Imperceptibly great peaks are moulded from the darkness until they gleam pale and cold against the waning stars. The light increases ; then suddenly the sun sweeps downwards in a golden tide. No poet suggested the beauty of a mountain dawn better than Tennyson :

> How faintly flushed, how phantom fair
> Was Monte Rosa, hanging there
> A thousand shadowy pencilled valleys
> And snowy dells in a golden air.

XXVIII

XXIX

XXX

XXXI

XXX. MONTE ROSA: DAWN

This photograph was taken from the Solvay Hut after a spell of bad weather, and depends for its quality on the lighting of clouds and sky. The camera is pointed directly into the rising sun which is just appearing over the huge massif of Monte Rosa, and a short exposure with a small " stop " has resulted in a thin negative but one with plenty of detail and contrast from the silver-tipped clouds to the dark troughs between them. The photograph is an example of relentless trimming as the enlargement was made from a portion of the original negative only an inch or so square.

XXXI. CLOUDS OVER ITALY

To judge from the clouds that day after day conceal the valleys of Northern Italy it would appear that the sunniness of this country, as well as its traditional blue sky, is something of a myth. Such clouds, when viewed from the higher peaks on the main watershed of the Alps, often make a striking background in a photograph, and in the present instance set off finely the snowy edge of the great snowfield in the middle distance. A filter is often necessary, but in this instance none was used and panchromatic film proved efficient by itself.

XXXII. EARLY MORNING ON THE GRENZ GLACIER

Early morning and late afternoon are the best periods for snow photography as the low angle of the sun reveals the folds, hollows and texture of the snow. This photograph was taken en route to the Italian summit of Monte Rosa an hour or two after dawn as is evident from the long shadows, and the texture of the snow is well revealed. In such photographs footmarks or tracks add to the interest and quality of the picture and it is the photographer's object to get them and any human figures in peaceful juxtaposition with the landscape; by so doing depth and distance are conveyed.

XXXIII. FROM THE ITALIAN SUMMIT OF MONTE ROSA

Panoramic views from the summit of a high mountain are notoriously unsatisfactory. There is nothing to arrest the eye which passes unseeingly over range upon range to the horizon. In such a case clouds are helpful to the composition, but the photographer should also try to interpose a foreground, otherwise the picture may resemble one taken from an aeroplane, and such bird's-eye views are unsatisfactory from a picture-making standpoint.

XXXII

XXXIII

XXXIV

XXXIV. THE RIDGE OF THE LYSKAMM

The Lyskamm is one of the finest snow peaks in the Alps and to traverse it is a classic expedition. This photograph was taken during the ascent of the north peak from the Margherita Hut on the Italian summit of Monte Rosa. A blizzard had recently swept the district and the snow had been blown by the wind into characteristic ripples which transformed an ordinary snow ridge into something subtly beautiful from the photographic point of view. It will be noted that these ripples form the motif of the picture, whilst the climber helps in the provision of a sense of scale which would be otherwise lacking. Furthermore, one of the most important principles in the composition of mountain photographs is evident in that the ripples lead the eye to a vanishing point out of the picture. This stimulates the imagination and at the same time aids the pictorial balance of the picture. Perhaps the ideal composition is one in which the vanishing point of the main lines is outside the picture and a secondary vanishing point inside ; the latter serves to eliminate any feeling of exasperation at being as it were cheated out of seeing more.

XXXV. THE MATTERHORN FROM THE WELLENKUPPE

The Matterhorn is one of the easiest and yet one of the most difficult peaks to photograph. It is easy because of its unique form which has inspired more shutters to click than any other peak in the world, and which cannot fail to be effective from whichever angle it is photographed, and difficult because of its scale, beauty and majesty. To convey these last-mentioned qualities careful attention must be paid to foreground which must not only serve to balance and harmonise the picture, but must by its lines lead the eye unconsciously forwards and upwards to the lofty tapering summit. Here is not a case for a " pretty pretty " lacery of pine branches—the stock-in-trade of the local professional photographer—but one calling for lines and forms almost as bold and free as the Matterhorn itself. For this reason I regard this picture as the best I have yet taken of the great peak, though I am well aware of its shortcomings and its woeful incompleteness : it is always a chastening lesson trying to photograph this most photographed peak. Yet, perhaps the fine sweeping lines of the nearer ridges and peaks serve to balance the photograph and at the same time build up the composition vertically by leading the eye downwards as well as forwards and upwards, whilst the gathering clouds add a suggestion of remoteness.

66

XXXV

XXXVI

XXXVI. THE MATTERHORN FROM BELOW THE COL TOURNANCHE

Seen from the south and west the Matterhorn presents an entirely different picture from that of the better-known almost symmetrical spire so familiar in photographs taken from the neighbourhood of Zermatt. It was up the south ridge, which lies on the Italian side of the mountain, that the early pioneers struggled in attempts to reach the summit, but these all stopped short of the Shoulder which shows prominently in this photograph until Carrel and Bich by a great *tour de force* overcame the final difficulties and won through only a day or two after Edward Whymper's ill-fated party had vanquished the mountain from Zermatt. The photograph was taken during a traverse of the mountain by an unusual combination of routes, first from the Schönbühl Hut on the Swiss side to the Col Tournanche and then over the Tête du Lion to the Italian Hut and so to the summit by the Italian ridge. The Col Tournanche is reached by an interesting and beautiful but not very difficult climb and the photograph was obtained from a point a short distance below the col. Finely moulded and brilliantly lit snow always makes an attractive contrast to a rock peak, but the great difficulty is to provide an exposure which will do justice to both. In the present instance I concentrated on revealing the snow, and the Matterhorn, as a result, is a shade under-exposed, though it may be that this aids its impressiveness.

XXXVII. THE MISCHABEL FROM THE SOLVAY HUT

During a traverse of the Matterhorn a party of which I was a member was overtaken by a blizzard and forced to shelter at the Solvay Hut which is about 1,500 feet below the summit.   There we spent two nights before the weather improved and this photograph was taken soon after dawn. It was a singularly beautiful morning with long brightly lit clouds suspended above the dark Zermatt valley, whilst a neighbouring crag in the foreground was a foil to the distant peaks of the Mischabel, the Dom and Täschhorn.   The most important point about a foreground in such a scene is that it helps the eye to bridge the distance and at the same time leads it downwards impressing upon it a sense of depth.   In mountain photography depth is best conveyed through dark tones and height through light tones and it will be noted that there is a range of tone in the picture varying from the dark valley to brilliantly lit peak and cloud.   In dawn or sunset pictures it frequently pays to aim at long panel-like photographs even at the expense of some ruthless cutting, though in this particular instance it was not possible to resort to this.

XXXVII

XXXVIII

XXXVIII. DAWN LIGHT ON THE OBERGABELHORN

This aspect of the Obergabelhorn is a favourite one with mountaineers and I remember several beautiful exhibits at Alpine Club photographic exhibitions. There is no more impressive ice-slope in the Alps than the north-west face of this peak, and long grooves worn out by sliding snow are reminiscent of the characteristic flutings on Himalayan peaks. The photograph was taken during an ascent of the Rothhorn by the Rothhorn Grat, one of the most interesting rock climbs in the Zermatt district, and two members of the party are seen on the firm granitic rocks of the ridge. The foreground is unsatisfactory ; there is something banal and muddling about it. Simpler treatment would, I believe, have resulted in a better photograph. Yet, perhaps such a shortcoming is compensated for to some extent by the background which calls to mind a still morning, with a frosty nip in the air and the prospect of a grand scramble. The photograph was taken on panchromatic film and no filter was employed. The stop used was F.11, and the exposure was 1/50 second.

XXXIX.   A GENDARME ON THE WEISSHORN

The Zermatt Weisshorn is one of the noblest of Alpine peaks and its snowy pyramid formed of sweeping elliptical ridges uniting in a point of mathematical exactitude is unsurpassed for beauty and gracefulness.   It was first climbed in 1861 by Professor Tyndall and the guides J. J. Bennen and Wenger, and Tyndall's description in " Hours of Exercise in the Alps " makes interesting reading.   There are now numerous routes up the mountain but the easiest, that followed by Tyndall, ranks as a fine climb and is arduous when conditions are icy.   Numerous gendarmes (rock towers) must be traversed on the ridge and it was from one of these that the greatest of all alpine guides, Franz Lochmatter, fell.   The gendarme in the photograph makes a fine foreground to the cloud-filled Vispthal and the peaks of the Mischabelhörner.   On such a peak it is not difficult to obtain photographs both dramatic and beautiful provided only a suitable foreground is selected, and when the valley is cloud-filled and the morning light at precisely the right angle the photographer can scarcely ask for anything better.   This is one of my lucky photographs.

XXXIX

XL

XLI

THE RANGE OF MONT BLANC

XL. MONT BLANC FROM THE MOINE RIDGE

Mont Blanc is not an easy mountain to photograph satisfactorily, for it is surrounded by subsidiary peaks and the valleys to north and south of it are so deep that from them it appears too foreshortened for its grandeur to be fully perceptible to the camera. It is best photographed from neighbouring ranges or one or other of the peaks or passes in the range. Next to the views from the Col du Géant and the Tour Ronde I prefer that from the Aiguille Verte, as seen from this direction the great mountain is admirably proportioned and a foreground of spiky Aiguilles contrasts beautifully with the swelling snows of the summit dome poised on its supporting buttresses.

XLI. THE MOINE RIDGE

Here is a curious composition. Yet, if there is no harmony and the eye is afflicted with an ugly wandering restlessness there is perhaps an unusual dramatic quality about it. In the middle distance is the Mer de Glace and Glacier du Géant rising towards the Col du Géant, whilst the queer spike of the Aiguille du Géant is clearly discernible. The rock formations are typical of a district which contains some of the most elegant pinnacles in the Alps.

THE RANGE OF MONT BLANC

MONT BLANC was climbed as long ago as 1786 by a chamois hunter, Jacques Balmat, and a Chamonix doctor, Michel Paccard. Much controversy has since raged over this ascent, due principally to the fact that Balmat, a braggart, afterwards belittled the part played by his companion. Mont Blanc, though a great mountain, is not an isolated peak but the highest point in a massif of peaks some 25 miles long and 10 miles broad. From scenic and mountaineering standpoints it is unsurpassed among Alpine ranges ; indeed a mountaineer might spend a lifetime climbing routes of all shades of difficulty ranging from easy snow trudges, such as the ordinary route from Chamonix to the summit of Mont Blanc, to climbs of Himalayan complexity and magnitude on the south side of the mountain, or gymnastics of the super severe rubber-shoe type on the elegant rock pinnacles of the Aiguilles which are grouped about Mont Blanc like Gothic spires around the cupola of a cathedral.

Much of the history of mountaineering thought and practice has been written on the range of Mont Blanc. From the days when the ordinary snow route via the Grands Mulets was considered a supreme and desperate adventure to the days when the younger school of climbers pit their lives against the northern precipice of the Grandes Jorasses may not be a long period of years but it has served to crystallize mountaineering ethics and habit. Great names are written over many a classic route : Edward Whymper who climbed the Aiguille Verte and effected the first passage of the Col Dolent ; Sir Leslie Stephen who crossed the Col des Hirondelles ; A. F. Mummery who first scaled the Charmoz and Grepon ; C. T. Dent the conqueror of the Dru ; Dr. Güssfeldt who opened up one of the greatest of Alpine routes on the Pétéret ridge ; A. W. Moore who first reached the Col de la Brenva from the south ; G. W. Young who climbed the Brouillard ridge, and a host of others. Nor must the guides be forgotten : Michel Croz, Alexander Burgener, Emile Rey of Courmayeur, the Couttets of Chamonix, Franz Lochmatter, Josef Knubel are but a few of many great names that crowd into the mind.

If I were to have unfettered choice of a mountain range where mountaineering par excellence is to be enjoyed I would not hesitate— it would be the range of Mont Blanc. The hardest climb I have ever done was up the East ridge of the Aiguille du Plan by the route discovered by V. J. E. Ryan and the Lochmatter brothers. Owing to snow-covered rocks J. H. B. Bell and I were forced to bivouac and did not complete the climb till the following day. Three thousand feet of difficult rocks, for the most part magnificent granite slabs and wonderfully firm—what more can the climber desire? Then there were two climbs on the south-east face of Mont Blanc up nearly 5,000 feet of superb mountain-side providing every sort of climbing on rocks, snow and ice : here the scale is Himalayan and the mountaineer enjoys as nowhere else in the Alps the joys of his craft.

Mont Blanc is a treacherous mountain for bad weather and, as befits its height, it is the coldest Alpine peak, though Monte Rosa runs it close in this respect, and many memories are inseparable from sudden storms, in particular thunderstorms. Of these last two were outstanding; the storm which overtook Dr. G. Graham Macphee and me on the Pétéret ridge and the one which occurred when Professor Graham Brown, T. S. Blakeney and I were bivouacking before attempting a route up the Brenva face of the mountain. Never, with one exception on the Schreck-horn, have I seen such lightning or heard such thunder, and in the latter instance we witnessed the extraordinary sight of streams of fire descending the Aiguille Blanche de Pétéret due to avalanches of rocks dislodged by hail and lightning grinding together.

Those photographers who are not mountaineers but are anxious to obtain first rate photographs of Mont Blanc are advised to walk over the grassy hills to the north-west and north or better still over the hills to the south in the neighbourhood of Courmayeur. From these the great mountain is revealed in all its grandeur, so much so that the camera will be hard put to it to reveal one tithe of its magnificence. Indeed I would say that there is no mountain range which calls for greater photo-graphic skill and none where skill and artistic feeling can produce such splendid results.

XLII. THE GRANDES JORASSES—SUNSET

The Grandes Jorasses is one of the finest peaks in the chain of Mont Blanc and has recently received much publicity owing to a number of attempts, several of which ended in tragedy, to scale its northern precipice which ranks with the northern faces of the Eiger and the Matterhorn as among the more desperate and unjustifiable Alpine climbs. Finally in 1935 the cliff was vanquished and the tale of disaster and competition, which had in it a most undesirable nationalistic element, ended.

Fortunately, however, such a view as this cannot inspire ignoble or tragic thoughts, for here is a great mountain in its most glorious mood with the sinking sun flushing its topmost crags above the clouds and a shaft of light illuminating the broken glacier far beneath, the one thing needed to balance the lighting and composition of the photograph. Confronted with such a scene the mountaineer must needs cast away from him all trivial thoughts and partake of the peace and beauty of the heights. The photograph was taken from the Couvercle Hut, a starting point for numerous ascents in this district and popular with visitors to Chamonix and the Monteuvers as it stands amid some of the finest scenery in the range of Mont Blanc.

XLII

XLIII

XLIII. THE AIGUILLE DE BLAITIÈRE

Height and steepness are best suggested by the lines rather than the angle of a mountainside, and opportunities frequently occur of photographing a mountain face on which long grooves worn out by sliding snow or falling stones are present to help the eye to assimilate the depth and grace of a slope. The Aiguille de Blaitière is one of a group of rock peaks on the range of Mont Blanc and this photograph was taken from the Grépon which is famous the world over on account of the excellent rock-climbing its firm granite rocks afford, and its associations with A. F. Mummery and his guides Alexander Burgener and Venetz, who made the first ascent.   The Blaitière is not so formidable and the climbing is largely over snow and ice.   The route to it, like the route to the Grépon, lies to begin with up the Glacier des Nantillons where hanging ice threatens the climber in one or two places; indeed it is a standing miracle that there are not more accidents.   On one occasion my party had the doubtful pleasure of seeing their tracks obliterated beneath three ice avalanches which fell an hour or two after quitting the danger zone.

XLIV. THE PÉTÉRET RIDGE FROM THE TOUR RONDE

The Pétéret ridge of Mont Blanc is the grandest and longest of the great Alpine ridges ; indeed in scale and magnificence it is Himalayan. It begins with the Aiguille Noire, the lowermost and sharply pointed peak ; then comes a group of pinnacles dubbed by some humorist Les Dames Anglaises, doubtless because of their forbidding appearance ; and after these the Aiguille Blanche, one of the most difficult, and certainly one of the most dangerous peaks in the Alps on account of its loose rock, yet appearing relatively insignificant beside its greater neighbour, Mont Blanc, which is out of the picture. There is no more impressive viewpoint in the Alps than the summit of the Tour Ronde, for not only is the Pétéret ridge seen in its entirety but also the Brenva face of Mont Blanc and the wall of rock and ice extending eastwards to Mont Maudit. Confronted with such a view the photographer may well despair. The photograph reveals but a section of it. The composition is assisted by the mountaineering party in the foreground. Here is an excellent example of the interposition of some human figures adding life to the picture and assisting in the appreciation of scale. The enlargement is from a quarter-plate negative.

XLIV

XLV

XLV. THE SOUTH SIDE OF MONT BLANC

To view to the fullest advantage the Monarch of the Alps you should climb one of the low grassy hills southwards of the Val Veni on the Italian side of the mountain.   Here is a view breath-taking in its magnificence and comparable with anything the Himalayas have to show. Rising well over 10,000 feet straight out of the Val Veni in buttress after buttress and peak after peak Mont Blanc lifts its final snowy point to a seemingly immeasurable height.   Three main ridges support the mountain, the Pétéret, seen on the right of the photograph, the Innominata in the centre and the Brouillard on the left.   Tremendously steep and broken glaciers descending between these ridges add their quota to a scene of extraordinary savagery.   Some kind of a foreground is absolutely essential when photographing the scene and the pines in the foreground add a bold touch to the picture and relieve the background from monotony. Remove them and the eye wanders aimlessly about, unable to discover a resting place, and Mont Blanc shrinks back into a uniformly monotonous plane.   Clouds relieve the background from uniformity, and I was fortunate to see and photograph the summit of Mont Blanc when it appeared for a few fleeting instants between them.

XLVI. THE COL DE FRESNAY

The Col de Fresnay lies between the Punta Innominata and the commencement of the upper part of the Innominata ridge which abuts into the face of Mont Blanc between the Pétéret and Brouillard ridges. The sharp, delicately curved snow crest cleaves into a background of low blue hills stretching southward towards the Paradiso. Many such views are to be had from the south side of Mont Blanc. The climber is suspended as it were in mid air. Above and below is the grandest mountainside in the Alps, and at his feet, separated from him by many hours of exacting climbing, the green pastures of Courmayeur and the Val Veni. Somewhat similar views are to be had from the northern wall of the Oberland whence the climber looks down on the pastures of Lauterbrunnen and Grindelwald, but none are more impressive than those from Mont Blanc with their contrasts of savage precipices, torn glaciers, dark green forests, and brilliant emerald pastures. The principal difficulty when photographing from such a steep mountainside is to discover a foreground.

XLVI

XLVII

KANGCHENJUNGA

XLVII. KANGCHENJUNGA FROM DARJEELING

The view of the Himalayas from the hill station of Darjeeling is world renowned. It includes valleys little above sea level and a summit 28,150 feet high. Kangchenjunga is fifty miles distant and the angle of sight is only a degree or two, yet it seems immeasurably high and forms a splendid centrepiece to a host of giant peaks that project like spurs of a foam-crested reef above waves of blue foothills. Early morning is the best time to photograph the Himalayas for soon after sunrise dense hazes frequently rise from the hot moist valleys and clouds conceal the peaks. A filter is essential, preferably in conjunction with panchromatic film, for the atmosphere is deceptive and details visible to the eye are liable to appear dimly or not at all on the film, whilst foreground is of primary importance. In the present instance the foreground was very carefully selected, but even so the conifer is a thought too heavy and tends to hold up the eye instead of leading it forwards to the central theme. In this respect the photograph provides an excellent illustration of the necessity for balancing foreground and background. Each must be complementary and neither must dominate at the expense of the other.

KANGCHENJUNGA

BEING interpreted, Kangchenjunga is said to mean " The Five Treasures of the Snow." This is due to the fact that it is not a single peak but a complicated massif built up of five principal summits, the highest of which is 28,150 feet, less than 1,000 feet lower than Mount Everest. Only a few days' marching is necessary to reach the foot of Kangchenjunga from Darjeeling and as the political difficulties are not great, though for some reason they are greater than they used to be, due I suspect to the large elaborate expeditions that have impoverished the Himalayan peoples during the past few years, several expeditions have attempted to scale the mountain during the past twenty years. Of these, only the Bavarian expeditions led by Paul Bauer have come within measurable distance of success and it cannot be doubted that the route over the north-east spur is the only one likely to prove practicable.

One of the most remarkable Himalayan expeditions of the past generation was that made by Douglas Freshfield and Professor Garwood in 1899, when they made a complete circuit of the Kangchenjunga massif. As a result of this reconnaissance Freshfield came to the conclusion that the best chance of success lay in tackling the north-west side of the mountain which is in Nepalese territory. His conclusions inspired Professor Dyhrenfurth with a desire to attempt the mountain, and in 1930 an international expedition of which I was a member set off from Darjeeling, having previously obtained political permission to traverse north-west Nepal.

After passing through the foothill country and traversing two snow-clad passes, the base camp was established on April 26th. A few days later the assault was begun via the Kangchenjunga glacier which leads to the foot of the north-west face of Kangchenjunga. It was at once apparent that Kangchenjunga is inaccessible over this face owing to miles of hanging glaciers which periodically discharge immense avalanches. Our one hope was the north ridge ; if this could be reached there seemed a sporting chance of success. To do so involved climbing over a hanging glacier which was patently unstable, but the risk was

92

accepted and the attempt made. Some days of desperately difficult ice work ensued, at the end of which time the route to a camping place on a terrace above had been almost completed. Then occurred catastrophe. A great portion of the ice wall on which we had been labouring broke away and fell on to the slopes below, where a large party of climbers and porters were ascending. A desperate dash to one side saved the party except for one porter who was overwhelmed and crushed to death.

After this the attempt to reach the north ridge was abandoned and an attempt to climb the north-west ridge was made. But this was a forlorn hope doomed to certain failure at the outset owing to the length and difficulty of the ridge.

We did not return from Kangchenjunga altogether empty-handed as four peaks were climbed, of which the highest was the Jonsong Peak, 24,344 feet, an easy if laborious mountain and not to be compared in mountaineering interest with the three other principal summits reached, the Ramthang Peak, the Nepal Peak and the Dodang Nyima Peak.

In one respect Kangchenjunga is in the same category as Everest. It can be said definitely that it can and will be climbed; perhaps this can be said of all the major Himalayan peaks, though there are some which appear impossible save by suicide standards. Most mountaineers will agree that it will be better for mountaineering when the restless ghost of altitude is laid and men settle down to enjoy the most marvellous mountain region of the world. Kangchenjunga and Everest have taught me that there is little pleasure to be gained in high altitude mountaineering or the fierce glare of publicity centred upon the major peaks of the Himalayas. The spiritual essence of mountaineering and mountain exploration is to travel where the spirit moves. To enjoy the Himalayas you must be free from elaborate " banderbasts " and newspapers, be within reasonable reach of the tree line and the flowers, and look upon the mountains not as national emblems and potential " records " but as mountains, each affording some new and delightful experience, some new problem to appeal to that curious and inexplicable desire inherent in man since he first trod this planet—the urge to tread untrodden ground. Everest and Kangchenjunga are duties still to be performed, but Himalayan *mountaineering* is a pleasure.

XLVIII. A FOOTHILL VALLEY

An immense range of climate and vegetation characterises the Eastern Himalayas. In a few horizontal miles it is possible to pass from hot, steamy valleys filled with luxuriant sub-tropical vegetation to eternal snows and temperatures below zero. Torrents of glacier water rush tumultuously along the foothill valleys towards the distant plains of India which they irrigate and fertilise, bringing sustenance and life to millions. This photograph shows the Rangit valley to the south of Kangchenjunga where it is little more than 2,000 feet above sea level. In the background clouds conceal yet suggest the Himalayas. Dense leech-infested jungles cloak the hillsides, and the hot moist air quivers to an insect chorus resembling the drone of innumerable saw mills at work and pulsates with the staccato clatter of frogs from every marshy place. Photographically, only the distant clouds with their promise of the heights lift the picture from the entirely commonplace. Clouds are often the making of a picture in which monotonous tones tend to predominate.

XLVIII

XLIX

XLIX. KANGCHENJUNGA FROM RINCHENPUNG

Our march to Kangchenjunga lay first of all across foothills, which gradually increased in height as we proceeded northwards. During this period the finest view we had of the mountain was from the Rinchenpung ridge. It appeared unexpectedly through the trees, a view so magnificent that it brought to mind Ruskin's peroration : " Out from between the cloudy pillars as they pass emerge for ever the great battlements of the memorable and perpetual hills." At our feet was a valley little more than 2,000 feet above the sea then, thirty miles away and far above the dim blue foothills, the summit of Kangchenjunga flanked by the square cut crest of Kabru. Already mists, formed from the moist vapours of the lower valleys, were gathering and concealing the peaks. The difficulty in such pictures is to strike a happy mean in exposure between foreground and background. In this I was not so successful as I could have wished and the foreground is under-exposed. A denser filter and panchromatic film—I was using non-panchromatic film—would have remedied the defect as well as rendered tone values faithfully.

L. THE BASE CAMP AND THE WEDGE PEAK

Professor Dyhrenfurth's plan was to attack Kangchenjunga from the north-west, so a base camp was established at about 16,000 feet by the side of the Kangchenjunga glacier. Opposite to the camp across the glacier rose the Wedge Peak. This, though 4,000 feet lower than Kangchenjunga, is one of the most terrific peaks in the world. It rises in a single precipice 8,000 feet high straight out of the glacier and is crowned by ice ridges so sharp that the sun may be seen glinting through their crests and fringing the peak with a cold fire. At intervals avalanches smoke into the depths and each hour produces some new combination of light and shadow on this stupendous monument of Nature. No photograph, however cunningly arranged, and this one makes no pretensions to be well composed, can do justice to such a peak. Conditions were disagreeable when we arrived at the base camp and snow fell persistently. The weather did not augur well for our attempt on Kangchenjunga which had been planned to take place in the short period of relatively quiescent weather between the ending of winter conditions and the onset of the monsoon.

LI

LI. CAMP ONE AT SUNSET

Camp One was at the head of the Kangchenjunga glacier near the foot of the north-west face of Kangchenjunga. It was in an impressive situation full in view of one of the greatest mountainsides in the Himalayas. Precipice on precipice and tier on tier of gleaming ice hundreds of feet thick, this side of Kangchenjunga shows defences formidable enough to daunt any mountaineer. I believe that no successful attempt on the summit will ever be launched in the face of its appalling difficulties and dangers, and that the only feasible route is the spur on the north-east side of the mountain which has been twice attempted by the Germans. Yet I am glad to have seen the hopeless side of Kangchenjunga for I do not suppose finer ice scenery exists elsewhere in the world. This picture taken at sunset shows one of the spurs of the great mountain looming down through slowly dissolving mists. To me, as a memory, it suggests the remoteness of the heights beneath which we struggled so hopelessly and dangerously before abandoning our attempt. To several of us who had been used to searching for the more difficult Alpine routes it was a humbling experience to be confronted with a peak with no breach in its miles of defences.

LII. THE ICE WALL

The ice wall on Kangchenjunga stands out in memory as the most dangerous place I have ever climbed. The only route affording the least hope of reaching the north ridge lay up a broken wall of ice some 400 feet high. In places it was vertical or nearly so and cutting a route up it was something more than hard work especially having regard to the altitude, nearly 21,000 feet. But it was danger rather than difficulty that made the ascent unjustifiable, for the ice on which we laboured day after day was part of a moving glacier and might collapse at any moment. I doubt whether greater risks have been run or more desperate hazards taken in the annals of mountaineering.

LIII. AN ICE AVALANCHE FROM KANGCHENJUNGA

The route had been almost completed up the ice wall when a section of the ice weighing tens of thousands of tons collapsed. Fifteen Europeans and porters on the slopes beneath had a miraculous escape, but one porter, Chettan, was overwhelmed and killed. After this the attempt to reach the north ridge was abandoned. Needless to say this is not a photograph of the fatal avalanche—we were too busy saving our lives to worry about photography—but of an ice avalanche from Kangchenjunga which fell towards Camp One. So great was the wind displaced by the falling masses that a moment or two after the photograph was taken the camp was swept by a blizzard of dust-like snow.

LII

LIII

LIV

LIV. FROM THE NORTH-WEST RIDGE OF KANGCHENJUNGA

Having failed to reach the north ridge Professor Dyhrenfurth decided to attempt to climb Kangchenjunga by its north-west ridge. It was not really an attempt as it was obviously doomed to failure at an early stage. To climb the mountain by this route would entail thousands of feet of ice and rocks of exceptional difficulty and a traverse of about five miles above 23,000 feet of which about three would be above 25,000 feet and would mean passing over two of the subsidiary summits before the highest was reached. Needless to say the attempt failed at an early stage. The crest of the north-west ridge proved to be broken into a series of huge rock towers which a strong reconnaissance proved impossible, if only from a transport standpoint. We were rewarded, however, with some fine views into the head of the untrodden Ramthang glacier. On the far side of this rose an unnamed ice peak, and I was fortunate to photograph it through a window in the monsoon mists which were by then crowding round Kangchenjunga. A projecting pinnacle from the north-west ridge made an appropriate foreground to a simple little photograph, which is impressed on my memory owing to an enormous ice avalanche which fell from Kangchenjunga a few seconds later. So terrific was it that the air displaced by the falling masses swept upwards and sent clouds of snow and ice particles into our faces.

LV. THE RAMTHANG PEAK

After the failure to climb Kangchenjunga a light camp was established at about 20,000 feet and from it Schneider and I climbed the 23,000 feet Ramthang Peak. We were able to ski for a short distance, then continued on foot. In spite of crampons a considerable amount of step cutting was necessary and progress was slow. It was wearisome for me, as in addition to my ordinary equipment I was wearing the special boots which had been supplied to the expedition. These weighed eight and a half pounds a pair and if crampons be taken into consideration, I was carrying a total load of twelve and a half pounds on my feet. The ridge leading towards the summit was typical of a Himalayan ice ridge. In places as narrow as a garden wall, so narrow indeed that there were holes through it several feet below the crest, it needed careful climbing to negotiate. The last slope to the summit consisted of soft deep snow into which we sank to our knees and we were both very tired by the time we stood on the highest point. The photograph, which was taken directly into the sun, shows the peak and to the left of it the glacier where the highest camp was pitched. The ridge over which the ascent was made falls towards the camera. The photograph depends for its effect solely upon clouds and lighting. It has been severely trimmed and but a fraction of the original has been enlarged.

LV

LVI

LVI. KANGCHENJUNGA FROM THE JONSONG GLACIER

After failing to gain lodgment on the north-west side of Kang-chenjunga Professor Dyhrenfurth decided to attempt the 24,344 feet Jonsong Peak as a consolation prize, which attempt was carried through with complete success. To reach the north-east side of the peak the Jonsong glacier was ascended and the 20,000 feet Jonsong La crossed. One advantage of this otherwise wearisome route (due to the moraine covered surface of the glacier) was the view of Kangchenjunga. For the first time we were able to appreciate, without having to allow for fore-shortening, the scale of the great mountain and the length of its ridges. There were often fine foregrounds to rejoice the heart of a photographer, and this photograph is one of many taken during the ascent. Four of the five summits of Kangchenjunga are visible, the fifth being out of sight to the left. Photographs which include ice and snow in both foreground and background are best taken through a filter, otherwise light and shadow are not sufficiently separated and the picture tends to become flat and dead. At the same time unless startling effects are desired the use of deep filters is to be deprecated as these darken the sky to an unnatural degree, though at high altitudes owing to lack of water vapour in the air the sky is a deeper blue than at low levels.

LVII. A CAMP BY THE JONSONG GLACIER

It is said of the Baltoro glacier in the Karakorams that the traveller, although treading the glacier, does not actually touch ice for several days and must trudge over miles of moraines. The same applies in a lesser degree to the Jonsong glacier and for two days after leaving the Kangchenjunga base camp we toiled over a wilderness of stone broken up into innumerable mounds which were anything up to 100 feet in height and frequently consisted of a thin layer of stones resting on slippery ice. At the second camp, shown in the photograph, the pinnacles, characteristic of the Tibetan climate, began and the moraine instead of being a curse became a blessing as it led us up between their ranks. These ice pinnacles afford many and varied opportunities to the photographer. In the present instance the camera is pointed directly towards the sun. The effect is dramatic rather than artistic, but dramatic scenes require dramatic treatment and the background of ice pinnacles is well brought out if at the expense of the foregound which is somewhat under exposed. The party were at breakfast when the photograph was taken and Irwin Schneider was probably setting himself up for the day's march on his favourite diet of Christmas plum pudding mixed with Worcester sauce and salad dressing.

LVII

LVIII

LVIII. SÉRACS OF THE JONSONG GLACIER

As the traveller proceeds northwards out of the moist climate that prevails to the south of the Himalayan watershed into the cold dry air of Tibet he notices a striking change in the nature of the glacier ice. On the Indian side it largely resembles that seen in Switzerland but ice exposed to the Tibetan climate is of a different character. Its peculiarity lies in the curious formation of the séracs (pinnacles). These attain a height and individuality unsurpassed elsewhere and the lowermost portions of glaciers bristle with thousands of immense pinnacles upwards of fifty feet high, the largest attaining to one hundred feet. These make striking subjects for the camera, though composition needs care, and the scale is always difficult to convey effectively. In this study of séracs of the Jonsong glacier careful attention has been paid to composition and scale yet the grandeur of the scene is not wholly evident. Only a colour photograph can convey the marvellous shades of blue and green that predominate in ice pinnacles. Correct lighting is another problem but experience has taught me that an oblique sun is the best when photographing ice scenery.

LIX. A CAMP UNDER THE JONSONG PEAK

This photograph of the Jonsong Peak was taken looking across the uppermost plateau of the Jonsong glacier. The mountain was not attempted from this side but from the other side where the climbing is relatively easy. When a large expanse of featureless snow is in the foreground the photographer is in something of a dilemma. He cannot eliminate the foreground otherwise no impression of height or distance is gained in the picture. Something must break up the foreground whether it be shadows, the most difficult of all details to arrange effectively, or human activity. In the present instance a camp serves to balance the background, indeed it tends to become the central theme in the photograph. The photographer must always decide at the outset what is to predominate as it is seldom that two main subjects can be introduced successfully into the same photograph. I speak from a pictorial standpoint only. The danger of including two climaxes is that each cancels the other out in a dead level of mediocrity.

LIX

LX

LX. ICE FRETWORK OF THE LHONAK GLACIER

Some idea of the great range of temperature in the Himalayas will be gained by studying this photograph. It is stated that sun temperatures of over 200 degrees Fahrenheit have been measured at 20,000 feet with a black bulb thermometer, whilst within the same twenty-four hours an air temperature below zero has been recorded. Hence the fairy-like fretwork of ice. The permutations in such ice scenes are infinite and it is easy to be led into taking ineffective photographs by sheer bewilderment as to what to photograph. Lighting, grouping and background are as important here as anywhere. Clouds, always good servants of the photographer, are often the making of scenes which tend to monotony unless there is something to relieve a hard background of sky—usually a deep blue sky in Himalayan latitudes—which reproduces too darkly when a deep filter is used. This picture like many others was taken without a filter, and though there is no doubt that a filter adds to the dramatic qualities in mountain and ice photographs, it often results in artificial pictures like flashlight photographs: many Everest photographs suffer from this defect. It should be the photographer's aim to reproduce not to dramatise Nature.

LXI. THE LAST PORTER IN TO CAMP

From a pictorial standpoint the photographs taken during the successful ascent of the Jonsong Peak were ineffective ; I have therefore omitted them as they are merely of topographical interest. One of the most effective pictures (to my mind) that I have taken in the Himalayas is this study of the last porter of the successful summit party returning to camp. We had had a hard time ; rations had been short ; we had been delayed by bad weather and some had been climbing for ten days without a rest. Here, a tired-out porter is trudging across a snowslope, his load on his back, a hard day behind him. The declining sun shining through a thin mist lights the crusted snow with a silvery sheen : altogether a picture with the simplest ingredients ; a rapid snapshot and a small aperture, nothing more. It was merely luck that the shutter caught the porter in full stride for it is difficult to obtain what you want in this respect. One simple little law of pictorial photography is evident : the porter is coming towards not going away from the centre of the photograph. Thus the interest is crescendo, not diminuendo—a point that must never be overlooked in photography.

LXI

LXII

LXIII

KAMET

LXII. FOOTHILLS OF THE CENTRAL HIMALAYAS

The foothill country of the Central Himalayas is very beautiful and to march through it is a perfect preliminary to an expedition on the high peaks. Forests of conifers and oaks clothe the hills, and villages nestle in the valleys populated by simple charming people. True, the flora is poor until the more Alpine valleys are reached but the colouring and atmosphere, and ever-changing vistas of green and blue hills, are delightful. The early morning is cool and dewy, the middle of the day and afternoon hot and the evenings cool. Frequently, thunderclouds gather and discharge their moisture in the afternoon freshening the air and charging the evening with the fragrance of rain and growing things. The photographer will do well to use a fairly deep filter and panchromatic film when photographing such foothills—deeper perhaps than was used to take this picture. This applies particularly to Alpine valley scenes in which it is usually hopeless to use an orthochromatic film, especially when distant mountains are included in the picture. For the rest, composition needs much attention if the picture is to be in the least effective. It is not effective in this photograph ; somehow it is muddling to the eye, and I include it only because it is representative of the foothill country through which we passed en route to Kamet.

LXIII. CAMP AT SEMKHARAK

It would be difficult to imagine a more delightful camping ground than this—a glade of springy turf set in a forest of Himalayan oaks and in the background the snowy peak of Nanda Ghunti.

KAMET

KAMET is a peak in the Central Himalayas 25,447 feet high. It is situated in the Garhwal district of the United Provinces and is the second highest peak in British administered territory, the highest being Nanda Devi, 25,660 feet, which was climbed in 1936 by an Anglo-American Expedition. The mountain rises in a single isolated pyramid from a glacier system close to the Tibetan frontier and because of its bold form attracted more mountaineers in attempts to climb it before the War than any other of the greater Himalayan peaks. The most success-ful of the pioneers was C. F. Meade who made three reconnaissances and in 1913 discovered a feasible route to within 2,000 feet of the summit where he was turned back by bad snow and the effects of altitude. He had discovered a sound route and it only remained for someone to complete it. After the War a new era in Himalayan mountaineering was inaugurated by a reconnaissance of Mount Everest in 1921 followed by attempts to climb it in 1922 and 1924. Meanwhile, yet another attempt to climb Kamet was made in 1921 by Dr. A. M. Kellas and Colonel H. T. Morshead, but like Meade they failed at about 23,500 feet.

In 1931 a small party of British mountaineers came together con-sisting of Wing Commander E. B. Beauman, Captain E. St. J. Birnie, R. L. Holdsworth, Dr. C. R. Greene, E. E. Shipton and myself. Kamet was our primary objective but as a secondary and scarcely less interesting objective we had the sources of the Ganges and the mountains of that district which bound the Gangotri glacier, the greatest Himalayan glacier east of the Karakorams.

From Ranikhet, a hill station in the north of the United Provinces, our route to Kamet lay first of all across the foothills of the Central Himalayas. Several hot marches brought us to the Kuari Pass. Beyond this are the high ranges and our way lay up the Dhaoli valley, a superb defile like the Lauterbrunnen valley in Switzerland on a superlative scale. The Garhwal Himalayas are indeed very like Switzerland—the same pine forests and fertile alps ablaze with flowers, and thousands of feet above the traveller immense rock peaks, the outposts of higher peaks.

After passing through a series of gorges we arrived at Niti, the highest village, where we reorganised our porterage and engaged a number of the hardy local Bhotias. After two further marches we established our base camp near the end of the Raikana glacier at a height of about 15,500 feet. To climb Kamet took a further two weeks. Five camps were established, two on the East Kamet glacier, one at about 19,500 feet, one at 21,500 feet and the highest near Meade's Col at 23,300 feet. The only difficult climbing was between Camps Three and Four, and from Camp Five a long snow-slope took us up to within a few hundred feet of the summit. Then came some ice and a slope which was a good deal steeper. The finish was along a sharp snow crest. The ascent took a long time owing to soft snow, and the cold was such that our Sirdar, Lewa, was seriously frostbitten. A magnificent view rewarded us on the summit, ranging from the peaks of Nepal in the east and Gurla Mandhata and the sacred peak of Kailas in Tibet to what we believe were the Karakorams in the west nearly three hundred miles distant.

Two parties made the ascent and we then descended to the village of Gamsali and afterwards crossed the Bhyundar Kanta Pass to the Bhyundar valley. This valley must be one of the most beautiful in the Himalayas if not in the world owing to the richness of its flora ; it is a natural garden and will always remain in memory as the Valley of Flowers. We remained two days in it then crossed another pass and descended to Badrinath, a sacred place to the Hindu pilgrims who journey in their thousands to the sources of the Ganges. The final stage of the expedition was exploration around the Arwa valley at the northern end of the Badrinath range during which we effected the first crossing of the watershed of the Alaknanda and Gangotri rivers.

It is impossible to imagine a finer district for mountain scenery or mountaineering than British Garhwal. It is also a photographer's paradise, so much so that photography is difficult owing to an *embarras de richesse*. Those who visit the Himalayas should remember that whereas exposures in the lower valleys should be longer than appear necessary the reverse applies to high altitudes. Films or plates should always be packed in airtight tins owing to the hot moist conditions that prevail during the monsoon season in the lower valleys and foothills of the Himalayas and the photographer must always provide himself with the newest possible stock, eschewing all film more than a few weeks old. Filters are advisable in the valleys but are not necessary on the snow if pan-chromatic film is used, unless for long range views or to accentuate clouds.

LXIV. AN OUTPOST PINE: KUARI PASS

The march to Kamet in 1931 took the expedition over the 12,000 feet Kuari Pass. Once over the pass the foothill country was behind us and before us rose the great ranges of the Garhwal Himalayas. A marvellous panorama was unfolded. Eastwards rose the complicated labyrinth of giant peaks which culminate in the naked splendour of Nanda Devi and the icy spear of Dunagiri. Westwards were the high snows of Gangotri whence the Ganges draws its strength, and set in this noble portal the range of massive mountains that culminated in the distant golden pyramid of Kamet. We descended into the resinous fragrance of a pine forest. The first tree we came to was a giant among trees, a solitary outpost gnarled and weatherbeaten by a century of wind and storm. Here, where the first spring flowers were decorating the firm turf, was the ideal resting place, and we sat down to contemplate a scene such as must have inspired the Hindu sage to write: " As the dew is dried by the morning sun so are sins of man by the sight of Himachal. In a thousand ages of the Gods I could not tell thee of the glories of Himachal where Shiva lived and where the Ganges falls like a lotus flower from the foot of Vishnu." At our feet was the deep Dhaoli valley, into which we must presently descend, filled with an opalescent haze. Beyond rose blue ridges lifting up and up like a succession of monster tidal waves to beat at last against the enormous buttresses of two splendid peaks, Gauri and Hathi Parbat, whose ice-encumbered summits gleamed at a seemingly immeasurable distance above the earth. What braver foreground could Nature devise than this solitary outpost of the forest with its sturdy trunk, strong arms and dark foliage ?

LXIV

LXV

LXV. THE NITI GORGE

To reach the base camp at the end of the Raikhana glacier to the east of Kamet the expedition followed the Dhaoli valley for several marches. The scenery hereabout, like much of Garhwal, resembles that of Switzerland but on a far greater scale. There are the same pine forests and rocky mountain sides, the same grassy alps carpeted with flowers, the same little villages with wide-eaved houses and the same gorges through which the melted snows rush towards the distant plains. Finest of all the gorges through which we passed was that just before Niti, the highest village in the valley. Here precipices several thousand feet high encompass the traveller, whilst higher still gaunt rock peaks seem almost to lean over the narrow track. The camera is hard put to it to convey the magnificence of such a scene but perhaps this photograph gives some slight idea of the frowning dungeon-like walls between which we passed before emerging into the Avalon-like glades of Niti. Sheer height and bold lines are the principal ingredients in the photograph, but light and shadow and the loom of a distant peak add their quota to the composition, whilst the scale is conveyed by some conifers which eke out a precarious existence in the rocky soil.

LXVI. CAMP FOUR AND MEADE'S COL

Starting from the base camp early in June the Kamet Expedition established Camps One, Two and Three without difficulty. Then came an awkward bit of climbing, rendered more awkward by snowstorms, but after several days' work a route was made and roped for porters, and Camp Four was placed on the crest of an icy bulge at about 21,000 feet in full view of the summit of Kamet and Meade's Col, so named because C. F. Meade was the first to reach it and discover a practicable route up Kamet. This col is 23,500 feet and it was hoped to pitch Camp Five on it and make a final dash for the summit. To reach it a gently sloping but considerably broken glacier had to be negotiated and the photograph shows the nature of this well and the apparent difficulty of the route. Actually, however, there was only one point where the least difficulty was experienced and the shattered ice could be avoided on the right. Such glacier photographs are best taken, as in this case, early in the morning or late in the afternoon when the oblique rays of the sun reveal the folds, cracks and joints in the ice, and the photographer should aim at a brilliant rather than a dense negative with plenty of detail in the high lights. Here, as in many other photographs in this book, there was no opportunity of arranging a careful composition.

LXVI

LXVII

LXVIII

LXVII. LOOKING SOUTH FROM 25,000 FEET ON KAMET

After a chilly night at Camp Five on Meade's Col, Shipton, Holdsworth and I, with Lewa our Sirdar and Nima Dorje a porter carrying photographic apparatus, left at 7 a.m. June 21st. Easy snow slopes led upwards towards the summit of Kamet and the only difficulty was the softness of the snow which made advance very slow and tiring. All went well until we were within 500 feet of the summit ; there we encountered ice and had to cut some steps. This was Nima Dorje's highest point as he was unable to proceed farther. The panorama was superb and the photograph gives but a hint of its extent and grandeur. Over the lower hills was stretched a vast sea of monsoon clouds, but the higher peaks stood out like islands.

LXVIII. THE SUMMIT RIDGE OF KAMET

The final slope leading up to the summit ridge was steep but not very difficult : the snow was in some places soft or crusted and in others hard enough to necessitate step cutting. One by one we reached the ridge, a sharp crest of snow, then advanced towards the summit, now only a short distance away. It was a superb finish to the ascent, yet we were a trifle anxious as not all the ridge was visible and we feared that an awkward gap might intervene between us and the summit. As quickly as possible we trudged along the crest. We descended into a gentle depression ; beyond was a snowy cone—the summit of Kamet. The photograph is a composite one—two photographs joined together. It shows to the right the top of the slope we climbed and, below, the East Kamet glacier where the first two camps were established.

LXIX. THE VALLEY OF FLOWERS

Following the successful ascent of Kamet, the expedition descended to the Dhaoli valley and after a rest crossed the Bhyundar Khanta Pass to the Bhyundar valley. The monsoon had broken and a driving wind laden with sleet and rain soaked us on the pass. Quickly we descended the far side over slopes of rocks and snow. The wind lessened and lost its sting, the air became warm. Suddenly we entered a kingdom of flowers. On every shelving ledge, by every rivulet grew great masses of a glorious blue primula. We camped amid masses of flowers. Next day we entered what I can only describe as an Eden of flowers ; we waded knee deep in flowers, the warm soft monsoon air was sweet with the scent of flowers ; our eyes wearied of the high snows rested on soft green and a multitude of shining colours made luminescent by the clinging drops of warm monsoon rain. It was the loveliest valley any of us had ever seen and it remains in memory as the Valley of Flowers.

We camped among dwarf rhododendrons, and that evening sat around a great fire with the stars looking down on us. Next day I took this photograph. It does scant justice to the beauty of the scene ; it cannot reproduce the colour of the rhododendrons in the foreground; but it was the best I could do. It was morning, and the shadows of the monsoon clouds beginning to form about the peaks lay like deep blue pools on the hillsides. In the background is the great peak of Hathi Parbat and beneath it an unexplored glacier curves out of sight behind a distant corner. A dark green sheet of pine forest covers the slope to the right with a huge tongue of avalanche debris beneath it.

LXIX

LXX

LXX. A FLOWER-CLAD ALP: BHYUNDAR VALLEY

The middlemost portion of the Bhyundar valley is an Eden of flowers. I feel I need only quote Holdsworth, the expedition botanist, to convey to the reader a picture of the scene. " Slopes of rich red loam provided a home for a thousand lovely flowers. Two dwarf rhododendrons ran riot, and in amongst them the Anemone narcissiflora grew in drifts of huge plants. Lower down we were to see it turn the hillside white four miles away ! Soon in stately groups, amongst giant boulders, shone the first flowers of the Kashmir blue poppy—Meconopsis aculeata —blue as the sky at dawn. . . . Rough alp gave way to lusher meadows, where among primulas, geranium and forget-me-not grew four choice bulbs (Nomocharis nana, Nomocharis oxypetala, Fritillary Roylei, and Lloydia Tibetica). Still lower down the valley, at 11,000 or 12,000 feet, we were over knee deep in grass and flowers. Here in the light shade of shrubs I found two plants of a rosy cypripedium (Cypripedium Himaliacum), and the purple cart wheels of a great aster (possibly Aster diplostephioides) peered up at us from the rank herbage. Two nights we camped in the lovely Bhyundar valley, and where we pitched our tents it was impossible to cut a sod of turf from the ground without destroying a primula or fritillary. For us it will always remain ' The Valley of Flowers.' "

The source of the Ganges is a region sacred to all Hindus. Every summer many thousands of pilgrims make their way through the foot-hills of the Himalayas to the pilgrim centres of Badrinath, Kedarnath and Gangotri situated to east, south and north respectively of the great range of peaks whence issue the main tributaries of the river. Of these tribu-taries the Alaknanda is the best known and is believed to be the true source of the Ganges. The actual source of the river is where it issues as a muddy torrent from the snout of the Bhagat Kharak glacier, but the devout pilgrim thinks of it falling from the foot of Vishnu " like the slender thread of a lotus flower." This telephotograph shows the Alaknanda valley only five miles from the source of the river. It is an impressive view with great rock cliffs forming a noble portal for the exit of the sacred water, whilst in the background are two peaks between 22,000 and 23,000 feet and a col, which has still to be crossed, leading over to the Gangotri glacier. The legends are innumerable and the mountaineer will find much to interest him in a district in which most of the major peaks are still unscaled. The Kamet Expedition made the first crossing of the watershed of the Alaknanda and Gangotri rivers and climbed several minor peaks. Since then explorations have been carried out by Marco Pallis and Shipton but much still remains to be done in a district of astonishing grandeur and beauty.

LXXI

LXXII

LXXII. A SLOPE ON THE AVALANCHE PEAK

The avalanche peak is an unofficial name given to a peak in the Badrinath range at the head of the Arwa valley where some exploring and mountaineering was carried out after the ascent of Kamet. It was a name given for a very good reason. We had climbed the peak without much difficulty and were descending the lower slopes which were covered with soft wet snow when we decided to glissade. During this glissade I started a small snow slip—it could scarcely be dignified by the name of " avalanche." At first it was nothing but a convenient toboggan on which to descend quickly and conveniently to the glacier but when I tried to stop I found the snow to be so waterlogged and heavy that I was unable to do so and I was carried ignominiously down the slope. All would have been well but for the fact that a bergschrund split the base of the slope which had an upper lip 20 or 30 feet high. Realising the danger I tried hard to stop myself, but the slip had accumulated to the dimensions of a miniature avalanche and I was borne irresistibly downwards. I shot over the upper lip of the bergschrund like a sack of coals and alighted heavily on the glacier. There the heavy snow compacted and for a moment or two there was such a pressure that I thought I should be crushed. Fortunately I was not buried and was able to extricate myself none the worse for my involuntary descent except for a cracked rib.

LXXIII. CAMP FIRE

Photography at night requires a fast film or plate and this picture was taken on an Ilford superspeed panchromatic plate the exposure being about 15 seconds and the aperture F.4·5. No flashlight powder was employed and the picture is absolutely untouched. To me it recalls a jolly evening in camp near the source of the Alaknanda river. After an exciting day during which one of our porters was swept away by a stream and nearly drowned, we pitched our camp on some turf and soon had a roaring fire of juniper going. It was a perfect night. The moon was making its way over the mountains between shawls of monsoon mist and the temperature was just cool enough to make us glad of our fire. For hours we sat yarning and smoking our pipes while the moon rose higher and higher, vying with the ruddy glow of the fire and shedding its radiance on the mountains, and from a distance came the constant rumble of the Alaknanda as it hastened over its rocky bed towards the far distant plains of India. I have only to smell the smoke of burning juniper to be transported to one of the most delightful regions of the world and live again the camp-fire life which, in some mysterious fashion, blends so perfectly the interests and companionship of travel.

LXXIII

LXXIV

LXXIV. NILKANTA: MOONLIGHT

What Siniolchum is to the Eastern Himalayas Nilkanta is to the Central Himalayas. We did not see it properly until the last evening before setting off from Badrinath on our return march to Ranikhet. All day it had hidden itself behind monsoon clouds, but after sundown the clouds melted away and between the dark walls of a gorge it rose full in the rising moon, a single tapering pyramid nearly 12,000 feet above us. As quickly as possible I screwed my camera on its tripod: I had no fast plates handy so was forced to use a relatively slow film and take an exposure of several minutes—I cannot remember exactly how long. It was pure guess-work but luck was with me. I even tried a telephotograph and this too was successful but the distant picture is the better as it gives a finer idea of the queenly beauty of the peak framed in the walls of the gorge. Moonlight photographs are often unsatisfactory as they have a knack of appearing like badly exposed daylight photographs and I have one of Kangchenjunga which is indistinguishable from a daylight picture. This view was a fitting climax to the expedition and its simplicity helped to engrave it indelibly on our memories. Perhaps in this respect the photograph is an example of that essential simplicity which is the secret of successful mountain photography.

MOUNT EVEREST

THERE have been six expeditions to Mount Everest and there is to be a seventh in 1938. Of these, two, in 1921 and 1935, were reconnaissances and the remaining four in 1922, 1924, 1933 and 1936 attempts to reach the summit. The highest point so far reached is within 1,000 feet of the summit, which is still officially 29,002 feet though independent surveyors have placed it a little higher. During the 1922 expedition the difficulties of the mountain were thought to be small, though the dangers of the North Col were realised when seven porters were killed by an avalanche, but in 1924, when Brigadier Norton was stopped at 28,100 feet by steep rocks, it was realised that they were considerable for several hundred feet, an opinion more than confirmed in 1933 when, owing to bad conditions, climbers did not succeed in advancing farther. It is now known that the crux of the ascent lies between 28,000 feet and about 28,400 feet and that if the steep overlapping slabs in this section can be climbed and the relatively easier rocks and snow of the final pyramid reached there is a chance of success. Success, however, depends on two other main factors, the weather, which is very treacherous on Everest and liable to give rise to sudden storms of hurricane force, and the altitude. As regards this last, it is perhaps sufficient to say that climbers estimate it will take eight hours to climb the last 1,200 feet of the mountain, whilst it has still to be proved that a man can live without some form of artificial breathing apparatus at a height which brings the atmospheric pressure down to a level well below half an atmosphere. Whether acclimatisation and physical fitness can bridge the gulf remains to be seen. Scientists are insistent that oxygen apparatus should be employed, but no lightweight apparatus which gives off oxygen for several hours has been designed, and both on account of this and because such artificial methods are abhorrent to most mountaineers it is unlikely that oxygen will be used in the near future save as a last resort.

The weather is the greatest factor of all and will always be a matter of luck. Both the 1933 and 1936 expeditions were cursed by terrible weather which never gave either expedition a chance ; indeed the 1936 expedition failed to get higher than the 1921 expedition, although its members were far fitter than they were in 1933, when 28,100 feet was attained. After climbing on Everest the climber may be forgiven if he feels as the superstitious natives once felt about the Matterhorn: " There seemed to be a cordon drawn around it, up to which one might go, but no farther."

One thing is certain, Everest can and will be climbed, it may be in 1938 or it may be a generation or more hence.

LXXV. CLIMBING THE NORTH COL

The steep 1,200 feet high wall of snow and ice leading to the crest of the North Col, 23,000 feet, is the first great obstacle that confronts the Everest climber. Up to nearly 22,000 feet the ascent of Everest is literally a walk, but the North Col has always been and always will be an intricate problem. It is simply a steep ice-fall which changes its formation year by year so that a route possible one year may be impossible the next and vice versa. Furthermore it is exposed to severe blizzards and in certain conditions the snow is liable to avalanche—as it did in 1922 when seven porters were killed. Owing to exceptionally bad weather it took more than a week to force the route in 1933, and blizzard after blizzard destroyed it when it had been made. In this picture porters led by Eric Shipton are ascending the slope known as the "Punchbowl" just below the ice wall, and the camera has caught something of the effort involved in climbing at nearly 23,000 feet with loads weighing about 40 lbs. It is a source of wonder to many that in the face of reverse after reverse the Sherpa porter will return undaunted to his task and always with indomitable cheerfulness. He is as keen as his employers that Everest should be climbed.

LXXV

LXXVI

LXXVI. PUMORI FROM THE NORTH COL

After ten days of considerable effort, during which period work was continually hampered by blizzards, the route to the crest of the North Col was finally completed on May 18th. The last slope was steep and icy and step cutting was necessary most of the way. One by one we popped our heads over the sharp wind-swept crest. The North Col was won at last. We congregated there breathing hard. Then gradually as our lungs ceased their pumping for oxygen in the thin air we became aware of the view. We gazed down the other side of the col to the head of the Rongbuk glacier, wrinkled and seamed by a labyrinth of crevasses, and beyond it to the glorious peak of Pumori, a queen among lesser peaks. Farther still was a tangle of peaks, unexplored and unclimbed, whence rose the mass of Gaurisankar, so often mistaken in the past for Everest. Light mists clinging to the peaks served to emphasise their height and steepness and revealed many a knife-like ice crest slicing downwards towards some glacier-filled hollow. There was little colour in this tremendous prospect ; it was hard, brutal, splendid, a dead world invested with blinding light.

LXXVII. CHÖ-OYU AND GYACHUNG KANG FROM CAMP FIVE

Camp Five was established on May 22nd, on the north ridge at a height of 25,700 feet. It would be difficult to imagine a bleaker and more inhospitable situation than the sloping shelf on the crest of the ridge, and it proved the most wind-swept spot on Everest. On May 23rd Shipton and I went up to occupy the camp in support of Wyn Harris and Wager whom we thought had advanced to make Camp Six. The weather, however, was so bad, that they had been unable to start, and as there was not room for another party they descended to Camp Four leaving us in position ready to continue with the assault if conditions proved favourable. Conditions did not prove favourable and for three days we endured the worst blizzards of our experience. This photograph was taken from the camp on the evening of our arrival when there was a temporary clearance, though the storm clouds are seen below ready to renew their violence at any moment. The scene was magnificent, but the wind so cold that it was impossible to appreciate it and the photograph nearly cost me frostbitten fingers, though my hands were only a few seconds out of their gloves. In the background are Chö-Oyu and Gyachung Kang, 26,870 feet and 25,990 feet respectively, two peaks to the north-west of Everest. Within an hour or so of taking this photograph a furious hurricane was raging. Our attempt failed and we were finally driven down to Camp Four with our porters frostbitten and unfit for further service on the mountain.

LXXVII

LXXVIII

LXXVIII. THE HIGHEST PHOTOGRAPH

Photographically and artistically this picture has nothing to commend it ; its sole interest lies in the fact that it is the highest photograph yet taken on the surface of the Earth. It was obtained from a point west of the great couloir at a height of about 28,100 feet. This elevation is the greatest so far attained on Everest and is shared by Brigadier Norton, who climbed alone to it in 1924, and by two parties of the 1936 expedition, Wyn Harris and Wager, and later myself climbing alone after Shipton had returned owing to illness to Camp Six. Some idea of the curious mental state of the climber at 28,000 feet may be gained from the fact that I did not remember taking it until the film was developed. At this altitude the climber is on his last reserves of physical and mental energy. His hopes and enthusiasms are sapped by an inertia which makes every upward step a mental as well as a physical struggle, and there is no doubt that the mental factor is as important as the physical factor on the last 1,000 feet of Everest. To some of us who are not fine physical specimens it is comforting and inspiring to know that there is at least one great problem left to mankind which cannot be solved by that brute force which is a feature of Western life to-day and finds its outlets in war, dictatorships and totalitarianism. Other mountains may be climbed by an application of mere force and skill but Everest will ever remain a pilgrimage of the spirit as much as an adventure of the body.